GEO. W. WASHBURN    RON

BEAR    ROU

JOHN H. CORDTS  NEW YORK

STEVEN CRYAN

# tugboats

# tugboats

## JIM SHAW

MetroBooks

# MetroBooks

An Imprint of Friedman/Fairfax Publishers

Library of Congress Cataloging-in-Publication Data available upon request.

ISBN 1-58663-039-3

Editors: Nathaniel Marunas
Art Director: Jeff Batzli
Designer: Dan Lish
Photo Editor: Kathleen Wolfe
Production Manager: Rosy Ngo

Color separations by Leefung-Asco Graphics Company Ltd.
Printed in China by Leefung-Asco Printers Ltd.

1 3 5 7 9 10 8 6 4 2

For bulk purchases and special sales, please contact:
Friedman/Fairfax Publishers
Attention: Sales Department
15 West 26th Street
New York, NY 10010
212/685-6610 FAX 212/685-3916

Visit our website:
www.metrobooks.com

**Front endpaper:** In this painting by tug artist Steven Cryan, a small flotilla of Cornell Tugboat Corporation tugs are docked at Roundout Creek, New York, in the 1940s. At the time, Cornell was the largest tugboat company operating on the Hudson River (covering the span between New York City and Albany), hauling everything and anything, but particularly coal and bricks. By the 1950s, Cornell was out of business.

**Back endpaper:** This Steve Cryan painting shows several of the New York Central tug fleet (nos. 31, 13, 15, and 35) at the main yard at Weehawken, where they took on water and fuel.

**Halftitle page:** The *Arthur Foss*, one of North America's oldest operating tugboats, rests in dry dock at Seattle, Washington.

**Title page:** The modern control console of the Mississippi River towboat *Patricia Gail* displays a host of electronic navigation and communication equipment as well as main-engine-throttle controls and rudder levers.

# DEDICATION

To William J. Oakes

# ACKNOWLEDGMENTS

I would like to thank (in alphabetical order) the following people, whose help and insights proved invaluable in the writing of this book:

Al Anderson, Crowley Maritime; Charlie Andrews, Crescent Towing; John Armstrong, Seaspan International; Darlene Bisso, Bisso Marine; Norman Brouwer, New York South Street Seaport; Charles Burrell, Leevac Shipyards; Todd Busch, Crowley Maritime; Chuck Cardinal, Oregon Maritime Center & Museum; Howard Clark, Crowley Maritime; Frank Clapp, Steamship Historical Society of America; Tom Coburn, Foss Maritime; Jim Cole, Elliott Bay Design Group; Steve Cryan, Steve Cryan Studio; Lynn Cullivan, San Francisco Maritime Museum; Brent Dibner, Tugboat Enthusiasts Society of America; George Duclos, Gladding Hearn Shipyard; Francis J. Duffy, Granard Associates; Nita Foraker, International Retired Tugboat Association; Kelly Francis, Washington Marine Group; Elizabeth Gay, McAllister Towing; Al Guidry, Quality Shipyards; John Hastings, Halter Marine Group; Bob Hill, Ocean Tug & Barge Engineering; Molly Hottinger, Hvide Marine; Don Hough, Foss Maritime; Dottie Hutchins, Cianbro Corporation; Len McCann, SS Master Society; Cullen Johnson, Newport News Shipbuilding; Eric M. King, Donjon Marine; George King III, Mystic Seaport Museum; Walter Kristiansen, E.N. Bisso; Matt Lyon, Harbor Images; Brian A. McAllister, McAllister Towing; Ted Miles, San Francisco Maritime Museum; Mark Mulligan, Robert Allan Ltd.; Mark Nichols, Nichols Bros.; Spence O'Grady, Marco Shipyard; Robin Paterson, International Retired Tugboat Association; Nancy Pearlman, Baltimore Museum of Industry; Aislinn Pitchford, Moran Towing; Ted Scull, Steamship Historical Society of America; Eli Shaprut, Voith Schneider North America; Sommer Shaver, Shaver Transportation; Mike Skalley, Foss Maritime; Glenn Smith, World Ship Society; Ralph Thon, Orange Shipbuilding; Hugh Ware, International Tug Enthusiasts Society; Carl Wayne, Tugbytes; Roger White, Edison Chouest; Jack Wilskey, Sause Bros. Ocean Towing; Trisha Wood, Mystic Seaport Museum; Dennis Zemvala, Baltimore Museum of Industry

***Above:*** Control fixtures from another era, a varnished wooden wheel and polished engine-room telegraph dominate the pilothouse of the historic steam tugboat *Hercules* at San Francisco.

# CONTENTS

# INTRODUCTION

This is one book about tugboats—it is certainly not the "definitive" text. It's meant to give a quick tour of the world of tugs: where they came from, what they do, how they're built, and where they end up after their working days are over. Tugs don't have the grace or stature of the sailing ship, the class of the liner, or the authority of the battleship, but they are genuinely likeable seafarers. Perhaps this is due to their size, or perhaps it is because, when they do work, they put all of their effort into the job. While the crews that man tugboats are a friendly lot and enjoy their work, tugboating is a hard and dangerous vocation. It's also a fatiguing one. Assisting big ships in and out of port can be stressful, particularly when a miscalculation or equipment failure can put all parties in jeopardy. Exhausting as well as pressure-filled, towing (unless part of a long trip) offers very little restful sleep. And a low boat in the ocean is always in danger.

The number of tugs in North America has decreased significantly since the late 1950s. The U.S. interstate highway system, built under President Eisenhower, has reduced coastal towing over the intervening decades, at the same time that the number of ships arriving in North American ports has decreased dramatically. New York Harbor alone welcomed nearly 15,000 vessels in 1960. Today, it's lucky if it sees 5,000 in a year. Modern container ships, some too large to pass through the Panama Canal, can carry the cargo equivalent of ten older vessels; tankers capable of carrying 15,000 tons (13,608t) of oil have been replaced by those with 150,000-ton (136,080t) capacities. Nevertheless, the tugboat continues to evolve as a flexible workhorse, one easily adaptable to new roles, and it is unlikely to fade from view.

Tug enthusiasts reading this book should treat it lightly. Hull lengths, horsepower ratings, and bollard pulls have all been rounded off, and there is no separation of indicated horsepower and brake horsepower. This is also a North American tugboat book. Except for discussions of early historical tugs, and the adopted "limey" sidepaddler *Eppleton Hall*, all the boats mentioned are from the United States and Canada.

*Previous pages:* A lone tugboat breaks the morning calm of Alaska's Resurrection Bay.

*Opposite:* Always at the ready, a tug and its crew wait for another vessel in need of assistance at Portsmouth, New Hampshire.

*Below:* A tug's pulling force is transmitted at the point where rope meets steel.

**Right:** The *Mathilda* heads toward the stern of the *Canadian Constructor*, tow line slack, beginning the process of turning the cargo liner around. *Mathilda* plied the waters of the St. Lawrence River for McAllister, Ltd., a Canadian tugboat company. Today, the *Mathilda* can be seen at the Hudson Maritime Center, a museum at Roundout Creek, in Kingston, New York.

**Below:** In this painting by marine artist Steve Cryan, the 112-foot (34m), 1,000-hp tug *Transfer No. 17*—operated by the New York, New Haven & Hartford railroad—can be seen steaming up the Hudson River past the Lackawanna terminal at Hoboken, sometime in the 1930s.

**Left:** Built at Newburgh, New York, in 1912, the eighty-foot (24.3m), 450-hp steam tug *New York Central No. 19* is captured here on canvas by painter Steve Cryan as the vessel's crewmembers go about their duties on New York harbor in the 1930s.

# FROM PADDLES TO PROPULSORS

To date, the history of the tugboat spans approximately two centuries. It started with the development of the early steam engines in Great Britain during the late 1700s. By 1801, a small steam engine had been installed in a craft called the *Charlotte Dundas* and successfully linked to a paddlewheel. This drove the vessel through the water and allowed it to tow several barges a short distance along a Scottish canal. Although the *Charlotte Dundas* proved a useful prototype, it made only one trip because the wash of its paddles, it was discovered, eroded the canal banks.

Over the next decade, other steam-powered paddleboats were built for towing purposes on less sensitive waterways. These early tugs became particularly successful on Newcastle's Tyne River, where sailing ships ferried coal to power England's factories during the Industrial Revolution. Although the coal-carrying vessels were graceful at sea, they were awkward in port, requiring just the right combination of wind and tide to enter and leave. The advent of the towing tug increased the efficiency of these wind-powered ships drastically, almost doubling the number of voyages they could undertake each year between Newcastle and London. By 1818, a number of towing tugs were active on the Tyne, and within a decade, the concept had crossed to North America.

The early paddlewheel tugs serving the Atlantic and Pacific coastlines of the United States and Canada were slow vessels with simple steam engines. They consumed voluminous amounts of wood or coal, and to keep fuel consumption as low as possible they were often rigged with sail. In this manner, they would sail out to sea to await the arrival of a sailing ship. Then, once a fee was struck between tug captain and sailing ship master, the tow would proceed back to port under a cloud of smoke. Although such a tow was costly to the sailing ship owner, the economic benefit of a quick turnaround time in port easily made up for the expense. A cargo ship could now enter and leave a harbor without having to wait for wind and tide, or for oar-driven longboat crews to handle its lines.

*Left:* A stranger afloat in American waters, the British-built *Eppleton Hall* is representative of the earliest of the sidepaddle steam tugs that first entered service in northern England during the 1810s and 1820s. The 1914-built tug was purchased by private interests in 1969 and brought to the United States under its own power. It was donated to the National Park Service in 1979.

None of the early steam-powered paddlewheel tugs built in North America survives, but a British-built steamer, the *Eppleton Hall*, can be seen at the San Francisco Maritime National Historic Park. Built in 1914, it is one of the last side paddlewheel tugs ever built and illustrates the design and engineering of these early boats. Its two independent, single-cylinder, vertically mounted engines are just up the evolutionary ladder from the very first steam engines built. First a working tug, then a pleasure yacht, the *Eppleton Hall* was rigged for an ocean voyage in 1969 and brought to 'Frisco, where she has since been maintained by the National Park Service.

The *Eppleton Hall* was originally built as a coal-fired vessel, but her steam boilers were later modified to burn oil, a conversion many early tugboats underwent as the new fuel began to replace coal in the 1920s. The use of oil diminished the amount of space required for fuel (stored in "bunkers") on a tug and increased its efficiency. Alas, the scent of coal smoke, once heavy in the air at such ports as San Francisco and New York, can still make early tugboat sailors nostalgic.

One of the few operational coal-burning tugs left in North America is the *Baltimore*, maintained at the Museum of Industry in Baltimore, Maryland. Built by Skinner Shipbuilding in 1906, the *Baltimore* is the oldest operating coal-fired steam tugboat in the United States and uses a compound steam engine, a type that began taking over from the earlier simple steam engines in the mid-1800s. In a compound engine, the steam from the boiler is first admitted into a small-diameter high-pressure cylinder, after which its (somewhat diminished) energy is reused in a larger-diameter low-pressure cylinder, resulting in a more efficient engine overall.

Besides its coal-burning power plant, the *Baltimore* has a distinctive hull built of wrought-iron plate, reflecting a phase of marine construction that predated the widespread use of steel in the early 1900s. Although many tugs were built of wood (a few as late as the mid-1940s), metal hulls were preferred if the owner could bear the expense. In design, the *Baltimore* is considered a "harbor inspection tug." It carries a longer deckhouse than would normally be found on a port tug of the period. The extra room was for local commissioners who required periodic tours of the port. While the use of municipal monies to build a dedicated touring boat might have been frowned upon by taxpayers, the addition of a few luxuries to a working, city-owned tug was considered a justifiable expense.

Despite its extended deckhouse, the *Baltimore* displays the classic tug profile that developed in the mid-1800s, when the propeller, or "screw," took over from the paddlewheel. The shift in propulsion yielded a stout-looking vessel with a deep hull, high pilothouse, and towering funnel. The propeller vastly improved the efficiency of the tugboat, providing more thrust. However, paddlewheels remained better suited to the western rivers of the United States because they were easily repaired and didn't need to be deeply submerged. Although it has not been recorded when the first tug master turned his boat around and used it to push another, pushing eventually resulted in two distinct tugboat designs: the general harbor tug, arranged for pushing and pulling,, and the larger oceangoing tug,, seldom used for pushing but capable of towing other vessels from port to port.

*Below:* An overhead view of the steam tugs of the Bronx Towing Line, owned by the Buchanan family, which hauled much of the sand and gravel that built New York City. Note the canvas over the stack of the tug on the left, a practice common among steamers to keep moisture out of the stack when not in use. The boat on the right, lacking a superstructure, is a stake boat, which was used at anchor as a holding point for barges bound for a variety of different destinations.

While the *Baltimore* is highly representative of the early steam harbor tug, the lines of an oceangoing tug are best seen on another of the San Francisco Maritime National Historic Park's vessels, the 150-foot (45.6m) *Hercules*. Built by John H. Dialogue & Son of Camden, New Jersey, in 1907, this boat is considered the last of the big oceangoing steam towing tugs built in the United States. In 1908, less than a year after its completion, it set a towing record by pulling its sister ship, the *Goliath*, from New Jersey to San Francisco via Cape Horn. For many years, the *Hercules* and the *Goliath* were two of the best-known tugboats on the Pacific Coast. When the age of the

sail passed and ships no longer needed to be pulled in and out of port, the two tugs switched their towing efforts to logs and barges. They survived for many more years, working along a coastline that was still largely barren of roads and highways.

Because of the formidable requirements of open-ocean towing, the *Hercules* was equipped with a 1,000-hp triple-expansion steam engine. Steam was produced in an oil-fired rather than coal-fired boiler. In a triple-expansion engine, the steam is progressively used in three cylinders (that is, one cylinder after another) before being sent to a condenser for return to the boiler as water. Although steam-powered harbor tugs could easily take fresh water from shore and didn't require condensers to maintain a supply of clean water, the use of such equipment on sea-going tugs was mandatory. The three cylinders of the *Hercules'* engine are laid out in a "fore-and-aft," or in-line, arrangement: each cylinder stands vertically, one after another. Shorter steam-powered harbor tugs often made use of compound "steeple" steam engines, in which the cylinders are mounted one atop the other. The iron-hulled tug *Dorothy*, built in 1890 and displayed at the Newport News Shipbuilding and Dry Dock Company in Newport News, Virginia, used a quadruple-expansion steeple engine, the first tug to do so.

Diesel engines began replacing steam engines during World War I, with the shift almost fully completed by the end of World War II. The diesel engine is a more compact and efficient power plant than the steam engine, and many an early tug underwent surgery to have the new engine installed. The first fully diesel-powered tugboat built in the United States was the wooden-hulled

*Left:* Bearing the long and lean profile of a deep-sea towing tug, the steam-powered *Hercules*, built in New Jersey in 1907, rests on display at the San Francisco Maritime National Historic Park. The white numbers on its stem indicate how far down in the water it's floating, also known as a ship's "draft." In this view, without fuel, water, or provisions onboard, the *Hercules* is drawing about eight feet (2.4m); fully provisioned for sea deployment, it would draw approximately 11 feet (3.3m).

*Chickamauga*, completed by Nilsen & Kelez for Pacific Towboat Company in 1914. As diesels don't require the tall smokestack of the steam engine, which requires draft for the boiler, Nilsen & Kelez routed the exhaust of the *Chickamauga* through side ports on the hull. However, in the eyes of ship owners, this removed the "powerful" look of the tug and most shipyards continued to add tall stacks to their diesel tugs, even though the structures were no longer functional.

While the early slow-speed diesel engines turned the propeller directly and had to be stopped and "reversed" before the tug could move astern, more efficient, faster rotating diesels were soon developed. These required clutching and gearing, just like an automobile, to reduce engine revolutions to a manageable speed that would in turn provide a way of reversing. Before marine gearing was fully perfected, these requirements could be met by using a diesel-electric generator to provide power to an electric motor attached to the propeller. The first diesel-electric tug built in the United States, the 105-foot (31.9m) *P.R.R. No.16*, was completed in 1924 for the Pennsylvania Railroad. As in diesel locomotives, a diesel engine was used to drive an electrical generator in the tug. The current developed by the generator was fed to an electric motor to

drive the tugboat's propeller. By regulating the current, the speed of the propeller could be changed, and by reversing the current, the direction of the propeller could be reversed. Although a number of diesel-electric tugs were built, their popularity fell off after the perfection of marine gearing because of their relatively high fuel consumption.

The onset of World War II brought significant changes to the tugboat industry. Besides forcing an almost complete shift to diesel propulsion, it spurred the construction of vast numbers of different classes of tugs, all built to meet specific military requirements. Although largely unsung, these military tugs proved vital to the war effort. One still afloat is the 114-foot (34.7m) *Major Elisha F. Henson*, which participated in the D-Day landings at Normandy in 1944 and is considered the only essentially unmodified example of the military's Large Tug (LT) class left in the United States. It is also the only known surviving U.S. Army vessel from the D-Day landings, during which its crew managed to shoot down one enemy aircraft. Built in 1943, the tug is on display at the H. Lee White Museum in Oswego, New York, as the *John F. Nash*, the name it was given after being assigned to the U.S. Army Corps of Engineers in 1946.

After the war, many surplus military tugs went on to swell the ranks of private tugboat fleets. In fact, these wartime vessels provided the backbone of the North American tug industry for many years. Nevertheless, owners continued to investigate new technologies in design and construction. This was particularly true for tugs used in ship-assist work, where agility was considered paramount. In 1959, the 100-foot (30.4m) tug *Dravo Pioneer* was com-

***Left:*** A classic portrait of a tug and its tow, the *Chas. D. McAllister* has taken a line from the American freighter *Washington*, which, without anchor, is being moved as a "dead" ship (that is, a ship without its normal crew and with its propulsion plant shut down). On top of the tug's wheelhouse is a ladder used by the pilot to board the cargo vessel. Built at Mariners Harbor, New York, in 1924 for the Atlantic Refining Company of Philadelphia, the *Chas. D. McAllister* was originally a diesel electric–powered tug but was converted to all-diesel drive when McAllister took the boat over.

*Above:* The world's first Ship Docking Module (SDM), the Hvide Marine–owned *New River* displays its unique profile at Port Everglades, Florida. Designed for in-harbor service along narrow channels and slips, the *New River* has a low, wide hull and a super-structure canted inward to avoid contact with the overhanging bows of ships being assisted.

pleted by the Dravo Corporation of Pennsylvania and fitted with a European invention, the Kort nozzle. This large metal ring, shaped like a wraparound airfoil, is mounted around a tug's propellor. Owing to the acceleration of water going into the nozzle, the pressure inside is less than that outside. As a result, there is a forward thrust on the nozzle and so on the hull. The installation of the Kort nozzle on the *Dravo Pioneer* boosted its bollard pull by almost 40 percent without any increase in engine

horsepower. (Bollard pull is a measurement of the thrust a tug can generate with its propulsion system and is authenticated by having the tug pull on a set measuring device.)

The *Pioneer* was also fitted with twin rudders mounted forward of the nozzle, called "flanking" rudders, as well as a traditional rudder mounted aft. The forward rudders provided control when the boat moved astern, thus providing exceptional maneuverability for ship handling. In time, the stationary Kort nozzles became free-moving and rotatable, allowing them to also function like rudders by directing the propellers' thrust.

While the *Dravo Pioneer* was built as a single-propeller tug, the advent of more compact diesel engines allowed the installation of engines side-by-side, resulting in more twin-propeller tugboats. A few owners also chose to adopt controllable-pitch propellers. These propellers contain a mechanism in the hub that allows the pitch, or "bite," of the blade in the water to be altered from the wheelhouse. The pitch can be "flattened out," or "steepened," to provide speed or push, depending upon the work requirement. It can also be reversed.

Two more inventions adaptable to tugboat design arrived on the North American scene in the 1980s. One was cycloidal propulsion, developed by Germany's Voith Schneider. The other was azimuthing, or "Z" drive, credited to Germany's Schottel-Werft, but traceable in this country to the linkage of engines, axles, shafts and propellers developed by the Murray Tregurtha Harbor Master Company in World War II. The first American tug to be fitted with Z-drive, the 65-foot (19.8m) *Tina*, employed Murray Tregurtha propulsion. *Tina* was built in 1977 by the Gladding Hearn shipyard for Delaware's Wilmington Tug & Launch. Z drive, which takes its name from the way in which engine power is first transmitted

***Below:*** With its mast folded down, possibly to allow passage under a bridge or to avoid contact with the hull of an arriving ship, a Moran tug glides past New York City's Battery Park in the dead of winter.

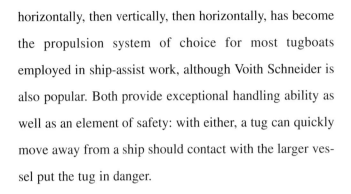

STEVEN CRYAN

horizontally, then vertically, then horizontally, has become the propulsion system of choice for most tugboats employed in ship-assist work, although Voith Schneider is also popular. Both provide exceptional handling ability as well as an element of safety: with either, a tug can quickly move away from a ship should contact with the larger vessel put the tug in danger.

The first tugs to be fitted with Voith Schneider propulsion in the United States were two 85-foot (25.8m) U.S. Navy yard tugs, the *Mascouta* and *Manasha*, both built by Jakobson Marine in 1966. These boats were later sold to private companies in eastern Canada and, like the *Tina*, are still in operation. A Voith Schneider unit is made up of vertically mounted blades that spin below the hull, something like an "eggbeater," but with the advantage that the angle of the blades can be constantly changed to provide hull movement in any direction. The concept of propelling a tugboat by using blades rotated beneath the hull can also be traced back to an American prototype, the "Kirsten experimental diesel tug" of the 1920s, developed at Washington State University. The Kirsten device worked to a degree, but only if the tug was operated backwards, an abnormality that quickly doomed it to oblivion.

The most recent innovation to surface in the tugboat industry is the Ship Docking Module (SDM), conceived and developed by Hvide Marine of Florida and Elliott Bay Design Group of Seattle. The SDM is a unique saucer-shaped tug developed for use in tight ship-handling situations. It employs two Z-Drives, one mounted forward on the hull and offset to the left of the keel line, the other mounted aft on the hull and offset to the right of the keel.

*Left:* The mood of early tugboating in New York harbor is captured by this rendering by artist Steve Cryan of the *Overbrook*, a Pennsylvania Railroad tug, escorting a coal scow past the Statue of Liberty. The tug's unusually large stack (the tallest in the P.R.R. fleet) inspired the captains of the fleet to nickname it the "Overstack." Other railroads employing their own tugboats during the period included the Delaware & Lackawanna, Lehigh Valley, Baltimore & Ohio, Erie Railroad, Long Island Railroad, and the New York Central.

23

This gives the SDM omnidirectional bollard thrust capability, allowing it to remain parallel to the side of the ship it is working, an advantage in narrow berthing slips or along tight channels. The world's first SDM, the *New River*, was built by the Halter shipyard at Lockport, Louisiana, and put to work at Port Everglades, Florida, in 1997. Well prior to this event, however, two similar in-line, Z-drive tugs were working in Prince Rupert, British Columbia. These hybrid craft were developed out of "shunter" units originally designed to assist ships in Canada's Welland Canal and were converted for harbor work by Prince Rupert's Minette Bay Ship Docking.

Despite the high degree of technical evolution the tugboat has gone through, tug owners must still choose their craft wisely. A Voith Schneider–propelled boat may be the best choice for escorting a heavy tanker to its berth, but the unit is expensive and its machinery complicated. Somewhat cheaper and simpler is Z-drive, but it is still a substantial investment. While both these propulsors make an efficient ship handler, they do not readily lend themselves to economical long-distance towing. For this reason there will continue to be a need for more traditional "shafted" boats that rely on long shafts and large propellers. A marine construction company or logging firm, in fact, can easily make do with a very simple tug. Maine's Cianbro Corporation, a marine construction company, has been operating its 67-foot (20.4m) single-propeller *Fannie J* for years. Although the tug is now on its fifth engine, its hull was actually built as far back as 1874, making it the oldest known operating commercial tugboat in North America.

# ON THE LONG LINE

The first tugboats were built for pulling, and many tugs today continue in that occupation almost exclusively. Small tugs can be engaged to move logs or scows, while oceangoing tugs can move barges and battleships. Steam-propelled side paddlewheel towing tugs were first put to use on the East Coast of North America in the mid-1820s and were active on the West Coast by the late 1840s. While the side-paddlewheel tugs survived for several decades in other parts of the world, they were displaced on America's East Coast rather quickly by propeller-driven vessels once the screw demonstrated its superiority over the paddle. Robert Bennet Forbes, who had made a fortune in Opium Clippers before developing iron steam ships and the screw propellor, teamed with the brilliant John Ericsson, the Swedish-born architect and engineer who designed the Ironclad "Monitor"

of Civil War fame, to launch the first twin-screw, iron oceangoing tug in the water in 1844. As the sailing ship era passed and the early tugs were no longer needed for towing ships in and out of port, they were put to work at other tasks. Barge towing was deemed particularly useful and it was a job to which the early tugs were perfectly suited: the early barges were often made from the hulls of obsolete sailing ships.

In the 1930s, after relatively high wages had been won by U.S. and Canadian seamen with the organization of the first seaman's unions, shipowners turned increasingly to the utilization of tugs and barges instead of conventional ships for coastal work. Towing a barge holding 10,000 tons (9,072t) of cargo might take a tug twice as long as it would take a freighter carrying the same tonnage, but the tug's crew of ten was much

*Pages 26–27:* A low boat on the wide ocean, a tug rises gently with the swells as it makes a deepwater passage.

*Left:* Under slack sail, a three-masted barque accepts a line from a steam tug for the long pull into port, sometime around the turn of the twentieth century.

cheaper than the cargo vessel's crew of forty. Today, although trucks and railroads have lessened the demand for coastal towing, it remains a cost-efficient means of moving large bulk commodities and is still used to move general freight to Alaska, Hawaii, and Puerto Rico.

## TOWING GEAR

Early tugboats did their towing with natural rope made from fibers of such plants as the banana (manila), Henniquin (sisal), and coconut (coir), but steel cable eventually became the mainstay of long-distance towing. However, for ship-handling and emergency salvage, synthetic fiber ropes are most often used. Some of these chemically produced ropes now have breaking strengths in excess of 500 tons (453.6t). Most long ocean and coastal towing is accomplished with high-strength steel cable measuring from 1.75 to 4 inches (4.4–10.1cm) in diameter, although the latter is most often found in heavy salvage work. The length of cable, or "wire," let out between the tug and its tow depends on where the tug is navigating and what the sea conditions are. A tow in congested waters, such as a harbor, requires a short line for maximum control, while at sea the line is let out to act as a "cushion" or "shock absorber" against wave action. The towline is usually attached to a tug's tow using a "bridle" made of wire and chain. As the speed of the tug and tow balances out, the line takes on an underwater arc, or "catenary," that hides it from view. This situation presents a constant danger in that other vessels may not take note of the tug's towing signals and attempt to cut across the submerged line.

**Opposite:** The forward deck of a modern tug supports a twin-deck winch, with hydraulically actuated drum brakes and spooling fairleads, all controlled from the wheelhouse. Both drums carry 4-inch (10.2cm)-diameter, 360-ton (326.6t)-strength Plasma synthetic towing rope. Unlike some synthetic ropes, Plasma line doesn't release energy in a dangerous whipping "snap" when it breaks, but simply drops. Mounted forward near the combined towing bitt/staple is a coiled messenger line, weighted with a special knot (called a monkey paw) that is used to carry the larger rope between tug and tow.

**Left:** Performing what has always been a dangerous job, a tug crewmember keeps tension on a 4-inch (10.2cm) line that has been carried from the tug's forward deck bitt, through a towing staple, around the bitt on the ship being assisted, and back through the towing staple. A misunderstood command, or the wake wash of a passing ship could suddenly exert too much pressure on the line, inviting a serious accident.

*Below:* An early car-float tug, wearing a traditional Golden Eagle atop its pilothouse, is guided through congested harbor waters by a crewmember standing on one of the float's forward boxcars.

*Opposite:* Backing off under a cloud of coal smoke, the steam tug *Chas. D. McAllister,* built at Tottenville, New York, in 1905, wears a traditional rope "pudding" fender on its stem but uses easily replaceable wood fenders along its side for car float work. (Note: The name *Chas. D. McAllister* was later passed on to a newer McAllister tug, the diesel-powered *Chas. D. McAllister* of 1924, shown on page.19)

# TOWBORTING ON THE HUDSON

It may seem odd now, but New York's Hudson River and its tributary canals, including the Erie, provided considerable towing work for early tugboats, much of it involving the transportation of building materials to New York City. Some of the big steam-powered tugs even carried passengers. Representative was the two-funneled *Geo. W. Washburn,* completed for the famous Cornell Steamboat Company in 1890. This 123-foot (37.4m) tug towed barges and canal boats along the Hudson while accommodating passengers within a long and well-furnished deckhouse. To make sure these travelers were not injured by the towline, it was attached not to the main deck but to the boat deck, one deck above.

Smaller "switcher" tugs, like the 1899-built *John T. Welch,* would meet the big towing tugs in midstream and add or subtract barges, transferring them to and from riverside docks.

A coal burner, *Geo. W. Washburn* could often be seen bunkering at the "coal pocket" maintained by its owners at Kingston, New York. Here, along with other contemporary Cornell tugs such as the *John H. Cordts* and *J.C. Hartt,* the *Washburn* would load coal, first through its starboard hatches until the tug was well heeled over to the right, then through the port hatches until the boat was brought back, pound by pound, on an even keel. While the rivers and canals provided natural, ready-built highways of commerce for the early towing tugs, competition from the rail roads and trucking

*Right:* Wearing a nicely woven stern fender, *New York Central No. 31* is caught on canvas by artist Steven Cryan as the tug's master shouts directions to an unseen listener.

*Opposite:* A small flotilla of Cornell Tugboat Corporation tugs is docked at Roundout Creek, New York, in the 1940s. At the time, Cornell was the largest tugboat company operating on the Hudson River (covering the span between New York City and Albany), hauling everything and anything, but particularly coal and bricks. By the 1950s, Cornell was out of business.

companies continued to chip away at the advantages offered by river towing operations. Eventually, most barge traffic disappeared from the upper Hudson and the old tugs were forced to serve out their later days doing piecemeal work in New York harbor. The *Geo. W. Washburn*, built in 1890, was eventually scrapped there in the late 1940s.

## THE PACIFIC COAST— SEEKER TUGS

On the Pacific Coast, the harsh realities of volatile weather and rough seas ruled out such refined craft as the passenger-carrying Cornell tugs. Instead, a longer, lower, and narrower type of towing tug came into existence. Famous was the 141-foot (42.9m) *Tyee*, built at Port Ludlow, Washington, in

1884. Like many sea-going tugs in the days of sail, the *Tyee* was considered a "seeker" tug, one that would go offshore to seek out arriving sailing ships to tow into port. The fee for this service was generally negotiated by the tug captain and sailing ship shipmaster as the tug maneuvered up close alongside the bigger vessel. Once a deal was struck, the line would be made fast and the two would proceed into port. At the time of its construction, the 1,000-hp *Tyee* was the most powerful tug in the United States and could easily work with the biggest sailing ships. It was employed within a pool of seeker tugs formed by various sawmills in the Pacific Northwest to guide sailing ships to their docks, until cargo steamers began taking over the trade after the turn of the century.

Other famous tugboats of the period were the 128-foot (38.9m) *Wanderer*, built at Port Blakely, Washington, in 1890, and the 110-foot (33.4m) *Wallowa*, completed at Portland, Oregon, in 1889. Although the *Wanderer* ended its days abandoned on the mud flats, as did many wooden-hulled tugs, the *Wallowa* led a charmed life. For nine years, it towed sailing ships across the treacherous Columbia River bar; then, when gold was discovered in the Klondike, it switched to towing supply barges to Alaska. In later years, it found work towing logs on Puget Sound. In the 1930s, after being sold by the Merrill & Ring Logging Company to Foss Launch & Tug Co., the *Wallowa* was discovered by Hollywood and in 1933 was used as the tug *Narcissus* in the movie *Tugboat Annie*. Perhaps as a reward for this role, it was given a new six-cylinder Washington diesel in the following year and rechristened the *Arthur Foss*. Eventually laid up in the 1960s, the old tug was saved and restored by volunteers and today is berthed at Seattle's Northwest Seaport. It is the last wooden-hulled, nineteenth-century tugboat still in operating condition in America.

## STEAM TO DIESEL— THE WAR YEARS

Like the *Arthur Foss*, most of the big towing tugs of the late 1800s and early 1900s were gradually forced to give up their steam engines and boilers for diesels once the new power plants became widely available in the 1920s and 1930s. World War II completed the transition, although it is interesting to note that the *Arthur Foss* was laid up for several years during the war because early U.S. Navy crews were not experienced enough in diesel to operate her. The war also produced an abundance of tugboats that entered private service once the war was over. One of the more famous war-built classes was the "Mikimiki" series, based on a prototype completed for Young Brothers of Hawaii in 1929. Some of these wooden-hulled tugs were built with twin engines driving twin screws, while others were built with single engines and single screws. They were strong, rugged coastal and open-ocean towing tugs and many remained in commercial service into the 1980s. Several, such as the 1943-built *Dominion* and 1944-built *Florence Filberg*, remain afloat as live-aboard boats in the Pacific Northwest.

Another class of World War II–era tugs acquired for long distance towing were the 157-foot (47.7m) Auxiliary Tug Rescue (ATR) units, built for wartime salvage operations. Representative of this class today is the tug *La Lumiere*, formerly the *Seaspan Chinook*, now retired from commercial service in British Columbia. This class of tug was built with wooden hulls and triple-expansion steam propulsion machinery to conserve war materials. After being declared "surplus to requirements" at the end of the hostilities, many ATRs passed into commercial service, most re-engined with diesel. In *La Lumiere's* case, this was accomplished using another war-vintage propulsion plant, a ten-cylinder Fairbanks Morse diesel acquired from the U.S. Navy's submarine fleet. Because of the submarine-style, sidestep gearbox arrangement, the replacement engine and transmission unit had to be mounted in the ATR's hull off-centerline.

The boat was kept on an even keel by mounting other equipment and machinery off-centerline in the opposite direction. For most of its working life, *La Lumiere* was operated by British Columbia's Island Tug & Barge as the *Island Monarch*, towing logs and barges along the Pacific Coast.

## MODERN TOWING TUGS

Today, such wartime tugs as the *Island Monarch* have been replaced by a new breed of steel-hulled, multi–diesel engined vessels such as the *Seaspan Commodore*. Operated by Vancouver, British Columbia–based Seaspan International, which took over Island Tug & Barge in 1970, the 5,750-hp *Seaspan Commodore* was built for offshore work in Europe dur-

ing 1974 but is now most often seen towing self-loading/self-discharging log barges. These barges use deck-mounted pedestal cranes to load logs from the water. The logs are then dumped en masse by ballasting the barge over to a sharp enough angle that the logs slide off, an operation controlled remotely from the tug. For long-distance towing, the 142-foot (43.2m) *Seaspan Commodore* can accommodate fourteen crewmembers, while its below-deck tanks can hold 110,000 gallons (416,350l) of fuel and 8,400 gallons (31,794l) of fresh-water. Once provisioned, it's capable of a 5,000-mile (8,000km) voyage under full-load conditions.

Tugs like the *Seaspan Commodore*, used for long ocean tows, are generally bigger than their harbor cousins as well as more sturdily built: many have a

***Opposite:*** Completed as a U.S. Navy ATR (Auxiliary Tug Rescue) during World War II, the Canadian-owned *Seaspan Chinook* was one of the last large wooden-hulled tug-boats to remain in commercial service on the Pacific Coast of North America.

***Above:*** Seen here working at full power, the 2,875-hp tug *Buckley McAllister* was originally operated under the name *Sea Racer* by Crowley Maritime, until it was purchased for the McAllister fleet in 1999.

*Right:* Leading a tandem tow of two deck barges loaded with oil-production modules bound for Alaska's North Slope, Crowley's 1976-built Invader-class tug *Ranger* heads north from Puget Sound.

raised hull, or "forecastle," in front for better protection against heavy seas. By necessity, they also have substantially more live-aboard space; larger fuel, oil, and water capacities; and higher-horsepower engines. They are usually equipped with a main towing winch, located about two-thirds the length of the hull back from the bow. The winch either supports several drums mounted side-by-side or a single take-up drum, which reeves (that is, draws the towline in, through an opening) and stores the line. Two winches can also be mounted one above the other in a "waterfall" arrangement. The use of multiple drums allows the separate towing of several vessels. The run of the towing cable is controlled by a "fairlead," set immediately in front of the winch, which helps guide outbound line and assists in realigning the line on the drum as it is spooled back in. To further control towline action, the wire may be guided by various posts and pins to keep it clear of the propellers and well away from the deckhouse in case the tug should have to work at an angle. Some older tugs also have raised steel arches called "strongbacks" across the deck to keep the cable well clear of other equipment.

## THE LONG TOW
## TO THE NORTH SLOPE

One of the most difficult long-distance tows undertaken in the western hemisphere is the movement of supplies and equipment to the North Slope of Alaska for the petroleum industry. This voyage is undertaken on an almost annual basis by several companies, principal among them Crowley Maritime Corporation of Oakland,

*Above:* The self-discharging log barge *Seaspan Forester* tips its 17,000-ton (15,419t) load of logs into British Columbia's Howe Sound after being towed south from the Queen Charlotte Islands by a Seaspan tug. Forest products—including logs, wood chips, and lumber—constitute the largest single commodity moved by barge along the West Coast of North America.

*Opposite:* Under snow-capped mountains bordering Alaska's Resurrection Bay, the inbound South Korean log carrier *Dooyang Glory* is met by an Anderson tug that will assist it into port.

California. Crowley is one of the United States' largest transportation concerns and its various subsidiaries undertake ship-assist work and long-distance towing along all three coastlines. It was established in 1892 and today operates a fleet of more than one hundred tugs and one hundred barges. From this fleet, it must choose equipment that is both sturdy enough and powerful enough to carry out the North Slope tow, a journey that passes through the Bering Strait, transits the Chukchi Sea, and enters into the ice-strewn Beaufort Sea. If the entire operation is delayed for any reason once north of the Bering Strait, the tugs and barges can be trapped for the winter, denying the company their use for many months.

A representative tugboat used by Crowley for the North Slope tow is the 136-foot (41.3m) *Ranger*, one of the firm's large Invader-class tugs. Between 1974 and 1977, more than two dozen of these 7,200-hp vessels were built by J.R. McDermott & Co of Morgan City, Louisiana. They are open-propeller, twin-shafted boats designed for long-distance towing, but are versatile enough for other jobs. One, the 1976-built *Stalwart*, has been specially equipped for tanker work in Alaska and fitted out with both emergency towing gear and fire-fighting equipment. *The Ranger* has a fuel capacity of 155,000 gallons (586,675l), and its two big General Motors diesel engines consume about 280 gallons (1059.8l) per hour. *The Ranger's* crew stays aboard for the entire round-trip voyage to the Beaufort Sea, which may take several months to complete. In the early 1970s, when the construction of petroleum-industry

equipment on the North Slope was nearing its peak, some 200,000 tons (181,440t) of equipment and supplies was barged northward each year, almost all of it during the ice-free "window" months of August and September.

## TOWING SHIPS AND BARGES

The towing of large "dead" ships (that is, ships without power or crew) requires considerable horsepower and endurance. Crowley has completed a number of these tows over the past few years. Difficult missions of this sort have included moving the battleship USS *Missouri* from Puget Sound to Pearl Harbor, the battleship USS *New Jersey* from Puget Sound to New Jersey via the Panama Canal, and the aircraft carrier USS *Oriskany* from San Francisco to Texas. Because of the *Oriskany's* angled flight deck, which would not fit through the Panama Canal, it had to be towed around Cape Horn, a journey of more than 15,000 miles (24,000km). By comparison, the tow of the *New Jersey*, which was able to squeeze through the Panama Canal with just inches to spare, was a journey of only 5,800 miles (9,280km). All three tows were accomplished by the same Crowley tug, 1974-built *Sea Victory*. This tugboat also gained fame in the salvage sector several years ago when it towed the bow section of the stranded Japanese wood chip carrier *New Carissa* off an Oregon beach. Designed for heavy offshore work, the 149-foot (45.3m) Sea Victory–class tugs are 13 feet (3.9m) longer and nearly 4 feet (1.2m) wider than the Invader-class tugs. Although they use the same 7,200-hp engines as

the Invaders, they have considerably more bollard pull but at a sacrifice of running speed. On the Sea Victorys, power is fed through lower ratio gears to highly skewed propellers enclosed in Kort nozzles. This results in a bollard pull of about 120 tons (108.9t) and a top running speed of about 12 knots. By comparison, the open-propellered Invaders have only 75 tons (68t) of bollard pull but manage a running speed of nearly 15 knots.

Crowley' s three Sea Victory–class tugs were designed to operate in extremely adverse weather conditions and have been given raised forecastles and heavier-built hulls than the faster Invaders. For towing purposes, the Sea Victorys are equipped with a primary tow wire 4,000 feet (1,216m) long and 2.75 inches (7cm) in diameter and a secondary tow wire 3,600 feet (1,094.4m) long and 2.5 inches (6.4cm) in diameter. The tugs also carry two 300-foot (91.2m) sections of nylon hawser for emergency towing purposes and a line-throwing gun that can throw a "messenger" line to another vessel several hundred feet away. (The messenger is used to pull a second larger line between the two vessels that will be used to pull over the heavy nylon towing hawser.) For the rigging of emergency tows, the flexible nylon hawser is both quicker and safer to handle. For routine tows, steel cable is more normally used. In addition to the cable, several "shots," or "legs," of chain, each about 90 feet (27.4m) long, are worked into the line to help take up surge action. In the case of the USS *Missouri*, the tow was made fast using 2.75-inch (7cm)-diameter wire in combination with several shots of 3.5 (8.9cm)-inch diameter chain. This was connected in a single leg bridle to the battleship's own 3-inch-thick (7.6cm) anchor chain, each link weighing in excess of 150 pounds (67.9kg).

Like many other tug operators, Crowley also undertakes routine year-around, long-distance tows of commercial barges, some moving between the U.S. mainland and Puerto Rico, others between Puget Sound and Alaska. The Puerto Rico tow normally makes use of Invader-class tugs, while the Alaska operation has been employing Sea Robin–class tugs. The latter vessels, built by J.R. McDermott & Co between 1973 and 1976, measure 126 feet (38.3m) in length and were originally powered by twin V-12 Alco engines developing 4,860 hp. These engines have since been replaced by Caterpillar 3606 engines developing more than 5000 hp. To give the boats substantial pulling energy, but also a good travel speed, power is transmitted through 4:1 ratio gearing, allowing the engines to rotate four times for every rotation of the four-bladed propellers. Four of these twin-screw tugs were built with raised forecastles for oil-field work, while the other four have low bows and are fitted with fendering for dual-purpose towing and ship-assist employment.

## NEW TOWING TUGS FROM OLD

Both the Sea Robins and Invaders have been the targets of major life-extension programs, demonstrating how older tugs can be kept economically useful over a long period of time. The reconstruction process takes approximately three to four to complete per tugboat.

First, the piping and electrical lines are disconnect-ed so that the vessel's deckhouse can be lifted off. The engines and gearboxes are then removed by heavy-lift crane and are given a complete overhaul and rebuilt. While this work is being completed, the tug's hull and superstructure is stripped and repainted. Once the paint has dried, the rebuilt machinery is reinstalled, the deck-house replaced, and all piping and electrical lines recon-nected. The result is a virtually new tugboat with zero hours on its machinery and a minimum of fifteen more years of service life.

## OFFSHORE TOWING IN THE GULF OF MEXICO

On the Gulf Coast of the United States, considerable towing is done for the offshore oil industry; most of it

is over a fairly short distance and involves supply barges and floating equipment. This requires a husky tug, but not necessarily one set up for long-distance towing. A modern boat fitting these requirements is the 90-foot (27.4m) *Thad A*, based in Cut Off, Louisiana. Built by R&S Fabrication, the *Thad A* makes use of twin 1,500-hp engines driving 7-foot, 3-inch (2.2m)-diameter propellers in Kort nozzles. To turn these large propellers with the engines putting out their maximum horsepower at 1,200 rpm, low 7:1 ratio gearing is used, the propellers turning once for every seven revolutions of the engines. This provides substantial power for towing, but limits the tug's top speed. The *Thad A* makes use of

"handed" engines, which means its twin diesels are set up to rotate in opposite directions. One can be considered "right-handed" in rotation, the other "left-handed." This balances the spinning force of the two propellers and prevents "creeping" of the vessel from one side to the other. Balance can also be achieved by using a reverse gear lay shaft, or idler shaft, which allows one propeller shaft to operate in the opposite direction of the other, even if both engines are set up to rotate in the same direction. Because its large towing propellers build up considerable turning inertia, the *Thad A* is equipped with brakes on each shaft so the propellers can be slowed and stopped quickly to allow the tug to be put

**Below:** A modern Gulf Coast tug, the 5,600-hp *Kimberly Colle* is as adept at moving drilling rigs as it is at moving ships.

into reverse. Most towing undertaken by the *Thad A* is oil field–related work within the 200-mile (320km) coastal limit.

The largest towing jobs in the Gulf involve the transportation of offshore drilling rigs and production platforms from one location to another. Moving these ungainly structures requires a team of tugs working in unison. When contracting for rig repositioning, the rig owner must provide the tug company with the platform's expected sea resistance. Based on calculations and impending sea and weather conditions, tugs will then be assembled for the tow on a basis of bollard pull or horsepower. One of the biggest offshore oil platform

movements ever undertaken in the Gulf required a massive amount of horsepower to go only a short distance. With a combined output of 70,000 hp, a team of tugboats took ten days to move a rig weighing 348,000 tons (315,705.6t) a total of only 250 miles (400km). To keep a rig moving, yet under control, a lead tug will generally connect to a wide towing bridle mounted forward, while other tugs will hook directly to the rig's own anchor chains. Additional tugboats will follow on stern lines to act as rudders, and a stand-by vessel will be kept available in case there is a mechanical breakdown on one of the other boats or a significant weather change calls for more horsepower.

## TOWING LOGS

Another difficult towing operation undertaken by tug-boats, but on a much smaller scale, is the movement of log rafts. Although the towing of logs is a declining trade, it is still practiced in the coastal areas of the Pacific Northwest and on several inland lakes and rivers. Log towing, in fact, has meant the salvation of many an older tugboat because high horsepower is not a requirement and there is little need for advanced mechanical technology. In 1971, Seattle's Foss Maritime completed one of the largest mass log-towing operations ever seen in North America when a longshoremen's strike closed down all U.S. West Coast ports, forcing suppliers to send their logs to Canada. On a single day, August 16, 1971, the company employed more than a dozen tugs to tow 376 log raft sections, the equivalent of 300 acres (121.2ha) of timberland, across Puget Sound. A single log raft usually has six sections, each section containing about seventy bundles of logs, and each bundle having from twenty to forty logs depending upon log size. As the rafts are only loosely chained floating log corrals, they must be moved very slowly, a task easily managed by a small tug of relatively low horsepower.

While tugs towing logs along protected coast routes and sounds must take wind, current, and tide into account, tugs working on rivers face a different problem. Although the tow downstream requires little horsepower because of the current, the non-revenue return upstream must be made as quickly as possible. To accomplish this feat on the Fraser River in British Columbia, an all-aluminum tugboat, the 34-foot (10.3m)

*Sea Imp XVII*, is employed. Designed by A.G. McIlwain, built by Sylte Shipyard and operated by Catherwood Towing, the 1,030-hp twin-screw aluminum tug is easily capable of controlling logs moving downstream at 2 to 5 knots, yet can return upstream at a speed of 22 knots. To achieve its high velocity in shallow waters, the *Sea Imp XVII* has a V-shaped planing hull with the propellers and shafting set in tunnels. The aluminum tug also weights just 16 tons (14.5t), less than half of what it would if built of steel. Because it can be quickly stripped down and transported by trailer, it can act as a back-up tugboat for Catherwood's lake towing operations.

***Opposite:*** With little requirement for great size or power, the logging industry keeps a large number of smaller tugs employed sorting logs and moving log booms.

***Left:*** Built of lightweight aluminum and using engines capable of developing more than 1,000 hp combined, the Canadian tug *Sea Imp XVII* can return upstream at a speed of 22 knots after completing a downstream log tow on British Columbia's Fraser River.

# PUSH AND PULL

In North America, a harbor tugboat is usually found pushing rather than pulling, although any particular job may entail both actions. Such all-around work requires a stout, well-protected vessel. In the prewar years, tug owners were continually examining new hull forms and enhancements they could make that would result in both a better-running vessel and one less susceptible to damage. In the late 1930s, the Curtis Bay Towing Company of Maryland, then under the command of Captain H.C. Jefferson, put the first two American-built Maierform design tugboats, the *Carolyn* and *H.C. Jefferson*, to work. In addition to the unique Maierform stem, which abruptly angles below the waterline to achieve less hull resistance and aid in ice breaking, these tugs also carried a broad steel bumper fitted to the top of the stem called a "war nose," an invention credited to Captain Jefferson that helped disribute the pushing force of the tug over a larger area of the ship's hull. Over this circular nose, built to help disperse pushing energy, a regular rope fender was secured.

In addition to the steel war nose and Maierform stem, the *Carolyn* and *H.C. Jefferson* were also fitted out with very heavy and deep steel guards to protect their hulls. These protective superstructures were integrated with the hull frames, extending along both sides from stem to stern. For muscle, a Skinner Uniflow 600-hp steam engine was installed in each of these tugs. The Skinner Uniflow, operating at 130 rpm on 185 pounds (83.8kg) of steam pressure, was acknowledged as the most advanced form of steam propulsion of the time, but even these magnificent power plants eventually succumbed to the superior diesel technology.

Thus fitted, steam tugs the size of the *Carolyn* and *H.C. Jefferson* could often be seen in New York Harbor nosed up against the sides of the great ocean liners. These passenger ships would often require up to five tugboats pushing on the bow and four more pulling on the stern to move them in and out of the docks lining New York's lower Manhattan.

***Left:*** Considered a pioneering tugboat in several areas, the *H.C. Jefferson* was one of the first tugs to be built with a Maierform hull, making it an efficient icebreaker. It was also given a steel "war nose," over which its forward fender was fitted, and a broad steel guard, which ran the length of the hull to protect against impact damage.

**Opposite:** Illustrating their value in shiphandling (not to mention their strength), two tugboats reposition a ship at its berth in Houston, Texas, so that the vessel's bagged cargo can be equally loaded into the port and starboard cargo holds. At one time such an operation would have required many more assist tugs.

In 1914, it once took fifty tugs to berth the world's largest liner of the time, the 950-foot (288.8m) Vaterland. The massive docking operation took place after the passenger ship was forced to stop in midstream because a tug and its tow suddenly cut across her course. With the big ship caught in an ebbing tide and strong wind, tugs were called from around the harbor to assist in moving her into the dock, an effort that took more than three hours.

**Left:** A big ship needs a big push, and Cunard Line's prestigious transatlantic passenger liner *Queen Elizabeth 2* routinely requires three or four tugs to safely "shoehorn" it into New York's Hudson River passenger terminal.

## THE RAILROAD TUGBOATS

While the Curtis Bay tugboats were designed for hard pushing with their stems and for taking heavy barges alongside, other tugs, including the famous railroad tug-boats of New York Harbor, did little pushing with their noses. Instead, they were almost continually lashed to "car floats," special barges designed to carry railroad cars. For this employment, they were fitted with side guards running the length of the hull. The guards were narrow originally, when the floats were made of wood, but widened in later years as float construction shifted to steel. Over these guards hung sacrificial fenders made of rope or wood that could be replaced when they broke or wore out. As car float work began to drop off because of tunnel and bridge con-struction, the railroad tugs were given fendering forward, usually made of rope, so that they could be employed in other trades. Most of these tugs carried high wheelhouses, some with an attached captain's cabin in the rear, while oth-ers were built with low profiles and squat funnels to allow them to pass under low bridges.

59

*Above:* This lineup of early Great Lakes tugs includes, from left to right: *Swaine* (1881), *Moore* (1865), *Sweepstakes* (1867), *Winslow* (1865), *Champion* (1863), *Oswego* (1861), *Crusader* (1874), and *Owen* (1875).

## GREAT LAKES TUGS

The tugboats working the Erie Canal and Great Lakes ports and adjoining rivers, where early bridges provided little in the way of clearance, were similar in their low profiles to some of the New York Harbor tugs. The first coal-burning steam tugs designed to work under these bridges were either fitted with forced-air fans or hinged stacks to ensure they had sufficient funnel draft for their boilers. Today, modern diesel engines have rendered the tall stacks obsolete, but some tugboats working in the Chicago area and on the Illinois River have hydraulically operated pilothouses that can be retracted when approaching a low bridge. Once clear of the bridge, the pilothouse will be raised again to give the tug master an unrestricted view over his tow. Many Great Lakes–based tugs were also given very large rudders to allow them to work effectively in narrow river channels where extreme lateral pulls were often needed to undock a ship or move a barge. On a standard 80-foot (24.3m) tug, these rudders could measure up to 8 feet (2.4m) wide by 10 feet (3m) deep, with a quarter of the rudder area suspended forward of the rudder post to act as a counterbalance.

## THE EARLY INDUSTRIAL TUGS

Besides towing companies and railroads, several other major industries operated their own tugs in the early years of tugboating. In 1902, a 91-foot (331.6m) tug, *No. 14*, was completed by Neafie and Levy for the Scony Oil Company (later to become Mobile Oil). For many years, this tug and many others like it assisted petroleum tankers and pushed oil barges around New York Harbor. Just before World War II, *No. 14* passed into the hands of the Meyle tug fleet and was renamed *Jupiter* for work on the Delaware River. Today, still known as *Jupiter*, the nearly 100-year-old tugboat resides at Penn's Landing in

*Below:* Under a cloud of black smoke, the steam-propelled tug *Wisconsin* pulls ahead of the newly dieselized tug *Maryland* in a race on the Detroit River, shortly after the Great Lakes Towing Company began converting its tugs from steam to diesel.

*Right:* Well-maintained, and now equipped with radar, the tugboat *Jupiter* can be visited at Penn's Landing in Philadelphia, where it is cared for by the Philadelphia Ship Preservation Guild.

Philadelphia, under the care of the Philadelphia Ship Preservation Guild. Although its steam power plant was replaced by diesel in 1949, the *Jupiter* remains an excellent example of the early East Coast "industrial" tugs that once numbered in the hundreds.

## THE "IRISH NAVY"

After World War II, tugboats began to lose much of their inner-harbor barge traffic because of bridge, road, and tunnel construction, which allowed trucks to take over most short transit work. Prior to 1940, more than 150 tugs were being employed to move 325 car floats in New York Harbor alone; the traffic could approach 76,000 moves per year. Today, there are perhaps four car floats left. The end of the car float trade and the retirement of the big railroad tugs has largely left the "Irish Navy" in charge of New York Harbor. The term refers to the big tug and towing

firms of Moran and McAllister, both founded by Irish immigrants in the mid-1800s. Tugboat stacks with the big white "M" (for Moran) have long been nautical landmarks along the East Coast. Likewise, the Red and White McAllister boats are known far and wide. Michael Moran formed Moran Towing Company in 1860 on the basis of a half-interest in the steam tug *Ida Miller*, while James McAllister followed a few years later by establishing the Greenpoint Lighterage Company in 1864. Today, Moran is publicly held as the Moran Towing Corporation, while McAllister has remained a family-owned firm operating as the McAllister Towing and Transportation Company.

## NEW TUG TECHNOLOGIES

Consolidation is an ongoing process in the North American tug industry as fewer tugs are required for docking and barge work. This situation has been brought about by a

*Above:* The well-known Moran Towing Company traces it history back to a half-interest held by Michael Moran in the early steam tug *Ida Miller*, seen here. The tug's doors are open for ventilation as it paces a three-masted schooner on New York City's East River.

***Above:*** A cold winter's day finds a Moran tug, fitted with raised wheelhouse for barge work, navigating through light ice on New York City's East River.

large number of factors, including more competition from railroads and trucking lines and the replacement of small cargo ships with larger ones. Tugs themselves have also been improved to such an extent that a single modern docking tug can do the work of several older ones. A major consolidation on the East Coast has seen the folding of the well-known Turecamo Maritime fleet into the Moran fleet, giving the latter company a roster of more than ninety tugs. By comparison, McAllister operates just fewer than sixty tugs. Both firms have invested heavily in new technology over the years to keep abreast of the latest trends in ship handling. McAllister purchased its first pair of Kort

nozzle/flanking rudder tugs, the *Brian A. McAllister* and *Teresa McAllister*, in 1962. These boats, previously operated by Moran, were developed out of the original U.S.-built Kort nozzle tug, the *Dravo Pioneer*.

## THE COMING OF THE TRACTOR TUGS

In 1986, McAllister christened its first Z-drive tug, the 104-foot (31.6m), 4300-hp *Brooks K. McAllister*, since renamed *Brooklyn McAllister*. The Z-drive propulsion system, featuring a ducted propeller that can, in most instances, be turned 360 degrees, has significantly changed the ship-assist sector of the tugboat industry by offering exceptional handling capabilities. The majority of installations of this type of propulsion on a tugboat see two Z-drives installed side-by-side, either in a forward position or in an aft position. General terminology within the industry refers to a tug with the former placement as a "tractor tug" while the latter is called a "reverse tractor tug." (Germany's Voith Schneider is credited with the term "tractor," used to describe how its tugs, fitted with forward-mounted cycloidal propulsors, responded to the helm just like a farm tractor responds to the steering wheel).

However, the term has since been embraced within the industry to include both cycloidal and Z-drive tugs. The tractors, whether cycloidal or Z-drive propelled, have become the leading choice for ship-assist work because of their rapid response and ability to aim thrust in different directions.

Well before McAllister joined the "tractor revolution," several other companies put smaller tractor tugs in operation. These included the two 100-foot (30.4m) twins *Brochu* and *Vachon*, as well as the 86-foot (26.1m) *Grand-Baie*, all cycloidal propelled and all completed for

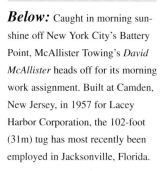

***Below:*** Caught in morning sunshine off New York City's Battery Point, McAllister Towing's *David McAllister* heads off for its morning work assignment. Built at Camden, New Jersey, in 1957 for Lacey Harbor Corporation, the 102-foot (31m) tug has most recently been employed in Jacksonville, Florida.

**Above:** Four tugs—including the *Roderick McAllister, Brian F, Eliot Winslow,* and *Marjorie Winslow*— take some off-duty time after attending to the needs of a number of warships. The outboard-berthed *Roderick McAllister* supports an interesting collection of fendering, including old tires, a section of traditional destranded rope, and compacted rubber strips.

Canadian mining interests in 1973. Eastern Canada Towing then had the cycloidal-propelled, 100-foot (30.4m) *Point Comeau* built in 1976, while Gladding Hearn completed the small Z-drive tug *Tina* in 1977. By the early 1980s, tractor technology had spread to the West and Gulf coasts with the 107-foot (35.5m) *Portland*, completed at Freeland, Washington, in 1981; the 78-foot (23.7m) *Charles Cates I*, delivered to Vancouver, British Columbia, in 1983; and the 85-foot (25.8m) *Mabel Colle*, finished at Houma, Louisiana, in 1985. By 1989, the 73-foot (22.2m) *Eleu* was working for Hawaiian Tug & Barge in Hawaii; and in 1993, the 84-foot (25.5m) *Stellar Wind* was completed for Cook Inlet Tug & Barge of Alaska.

Most of these ship-handling tractor tugs adopted new elements of tug design and engineering that had been progressively developed through the 1970s. This included pilothouse windows slanted inwards to minimize glare, pilothouse "eyebrow" viewing ports to enable the tug master to view upwards, and deck winches that could be remotely controlled from the pilothouse. The pilothouse itself was gradually moved to a more centered position on the hull and narrowed to protect it from damage while the tug worked ships with highly flared bows.

The first large-scale order for series-built tractor tug technology came in 1981, when Seattle, Washington–based Foss Maritime ordered six cycloidal-propelled tugs from Tacoma Boatbuilding Company of Tacoma, Washington. These tugs—the 106-foot (32.2m), 4000-hp *Andrew Foss* and *Arthur Foss* and the 100-foot (30.4m), 3000-hp W*edell Foss*, *Henry Foss*, *Pacific Tractor*, and *Pacific Escort*—were the result of new state and federal regulations requiring tug escorting of tankers of more than 40,000 deadweight (dwt) in Puget Sound, as well as the continuing growth in size of container ships and car-carrying vessels. Built at a cost of $5 million each, the new Foss tugs were given German-designed Voith Schneider propulsion units. These propulsors have five vertically mounted blades that stand 79 inches (2m) high and orbit in a diameter of 10 feet, 6 inches (3.1m) under the

tug's hull. The controllable-pitch blades provide thrust and steering in all directions at a constant engine rpm, allowing tremendous maneuverability as well as promoting long engine life.

Since the Foss order, a growing number of tugboat operators have become members of the tractor fraternity, with Florida's Hvide Marine and Cleveland's Great Lakes Towing both making series orders and each choosing Z-drive propulsion. All of these tugs mount the units in the stern except for Hvide's first tractor, the 1995-built *Broward*, which was designed by the Elliott Bay Design Group of Seattle to have its propulsion unit forward. Hvide and Elliott Bay also teamed up to develop the Ship

**Below:** Running at speed, the Turecamo Maritime tug *Turecamo Girls* dashes past the New York waterfront on a mid-afternoon assignment. Since the incorporation of the Turecamo fleet into the Moran fleet, the wood-grain finish applied to the pilothouses of some Turecamo tugs has been painted over in Moran colors.

*Above:* One of the most modern boats in the Moran fleet, yet still making use of rope fendering, the 4,200-hp *Karen Moran* is one of a series of six new Z-drive tugs designed and built by Washburn & Doughty (of East Boothbay, Maine) for the handling of U.S. Navy ships. It is similar in size to a series of Z-drive tugs built for Great Lakes Towing and is employed in a program that is seeing the gradual replacement of U.S. Navy tugs by privately owned tugboats operating under long-term contract.

*Opposite:* Giving away the forward position of its Z-drive propulsion units, Hvide Marine's tug *Broward* demonstrates its agility at Port Everglades, Florida, by spinning on its own axis.

Docking Module (SDM), which uses two Z-drives that are mounted on the hull, diagonally offset 6 feet, 6 inches (1.9m) from the centerline; one propulsor is located near the bow and the other near the stern. This allows the 90-foot-by-50-foot (27.3 by 15.2m) SDM to provide 100 percent of its pushing or pulling forces in any direction, giving it the maneuverability to work in constrictive harbor situations; by the same token, it is not designed to go to sea.

Great Lakes Towing, the largest tugboat operator on the Great Lakes, has had five Z-drive tractor tugs built by Halter Marine in Mississippi and the Marco Shipyard in Washington, although none is in service on the Great Lakes. Instead, they are employed under a program that is seeing the gradual replacement of most U.S. Navy harbor tugs by privately owned tugboats working under long-term

contracts. All five of the 94-foot (28.5m) Great Lakes Z-drive tugs, known as the *Z-One, Z-Two, Z-Three, Z-Four,* and *Z-Five,* were specially designed for U.S. Navy work by Jensen Maritime Consultants of Seattle. These tugs are equipped with rubber fendering above and below water to allow them to safely work submarines as well as assist larger vessels. In stature, the five Z tugs are substantially different from Great Lakes Towing's traditional low-profile tugs, which were developed more than a century ago to move under bridges at Great Lakes ports. Some of these low-profile tugs, with their distinctive red and white paint and white "G" on the funnel, have worked along the Gulf of Mexico.

## GULF COAST TUGBOATS

Gulf Coast tugboat companies have been somewhat slower than their East and West coast counterparts to embrace new tractor tug technology. Only recently have such firms as Crescent Towing and Bisso Towboat Company ordered tractor tugs. Crescent now has within its fleet the 105-foot (31.9m) *Point Clear,* delivered by the Thoma-Sea Shipyard in 1999, while Bisso operates the 100-foot (30.4m) *Cecilia B. Slatten,* completed by Main Iron Works in 1999. Crescent Towing is a subsidiary of stevedoring company Cooper/T. Smith and was founded during World War II to move derrick barges on the Mississippi, while Bisso Towboat was formed by Captain Joseph Bisso in 1880 around an early cross-river ferry service. The *Point Clear* makes use of twin 2,500-hp engines coupled to twin Z-drives to generate a bollard pull

**Above:** A tugboat that goes by number rather than name, the *C-Tractor 8* is a 90-foot (27.4m), 2,400-hp Z-drive tug operated by Edison Chouest of Galliano, Louisiana. Designed to assist large U.S. Navy ships at the Port of San Diego, it carries fendered "wings" on each side of the wheelhouse to help transfer pushing energy and to prevent "tripping" (excessive heeling) as the tug works alongside the larger vessel while underway.

of 72.5 tons (65.8t), while the 3,900-hp *Cecilia B. Slatten* (first Z-drive tug to be specifically designed and constructed to operate on the Mississippi River) generates about 58.5 tons (53.1t) of bollard pull.

Another Mississippi tugboat operator is E.N. Bisso, which traces its history back to the same Captain Joseph Bisso of Bisso Towboat, but today operates as a separate company. Although Bisso Towboat elected to go with Z-drive for its latest ship-handling tug, E.N. Bisso has remained with a more conventional design. Its newest boat, the 105-foot (31.9m) *Vera Bisso*, makes use of twin propellers enclosed in Kort nozzles with main and flanking

rudders. While not quite as agile as the reverse tractor *Cecilia B. Slatten*, the *Vera Bisso's* bollard-pull-to-horsepower ratio, at 67.5 tons (61.2t)/3,900 hp, is greater. This is because of the 11-foot, 6-inch (3.5m)-diameter propellers the *Vera* employs compared to the *Slatten's* 7-foot, 6-inch (2.3m)-diameter propellers. However, the *Vera Bisso's* bollard pull drops off substantially when the tug is operated in reverse because its propeller blades are pitched for forward movement. The *Cecilia B. Slatten*, by contrast, has a more constant bollard pull because its whole propeller mechanism can be reversed, the blades continuing to bite into the water at the same pitch.

## SHALLOW WATER TUGS

Shallow water operation, such as on the upper reaches of the Mississippi River, presents a difficult assignment for a tugboat as its propulsion system must be well submerged at all times to achieve full power. To gain the same blade-to-water contact area that a deepwater boat will have using two large propellers, a shallow water tug may employ three smaller propellers. Such a vessel is the 72-foot (21.8m) *Connor A. Gisclair*, built by Rodriguez Boat Builders of Bayou La Batre, Louisiana, for Inshore Marine, Inc. This tug has three diesel engines of 350 hp driving three heavily pitched propellers working inside nozzles that are themselves recessed into tear-shaped sections of the hull. The outside diameter of the nozzles is only 5 feet (1.5m), allowing the *Connor A. Gisclair* to float on a working draft of 6 feet, 6 inches (1.9m). Although the tug usually works on the river, it can be ballasted down to 8 feet, 6 inches (2.6m) to give it more stability if it works in outside waters.

## MISSISSIPPI TOWBOATS

While the *Connor A. Gisclair* has a "model" hull, with rounded bows forward, and looks like a traditional tugboat,

*Below:* Protected by a string of tires rather than continuous rubber fendering, the tug *Cecilia B. Slatten*, built with twin Z-drive units mounted under the stern, gets underway on the Mississippi River.

*Pages 72–73:* Built for ship-assist work, as well as pushing and towing, the 105-foot (40.2m) Mississippi River tug *Vera Bisso* carries deck winches fore and aft and has been fitted with a broad pushing fender forward as well as a high-visibility wheelhouse.

*Right:* Making the turn at Algiers Point in New Orleans, a lone towboat proceeds past a second boat pushing a multi-barge tow. The lower Mississippi is one of the world's most difficult and congested stretches of water to navigate and it is at this writing coming under the control of a computer and radar-based Vessel Management System operated by the U.S. Coast Guard.

*Opposite, top:* The 8,000-hp towboat *Patricia Gail*, operated by Memco Barge Line of St. Louis, Missouri, makes its way through river mist shortly after being completed by Quality Shipyards of Houma, Louisiana.

*Opposite, bottom:* Looking as "boxy" as the barges they are attending, a collection of square-hulled pushboats works up a train of Lighter Aboard Ship (LASH) barges on the Mississippi River. LASH barges, built to uniform measurements, are carried aboard special LASH vessels, which are equipped with large, stern-mounted gantry cranes capable of lifting and lowering the barges.

many vessels working along the Intercoastal Waterway and on the inland river systems are rectangular in shape, with blunt noses suitable for pushing. Although some of these "towboats" might be used for occasional ship handling, the majority are employed to move barges. On the Mississippi, some barge tows can exceed sixty units and require a towboat of up to 15,000 hp for propulsion. On the narrower Gulf Intercoastal Waterway, which stretches 1,065 miles (1,704km) from Carabelle, Florida, to Brownsville, Texas, a two-barge tow and a much smaller horsepower requirement is common. One of the newest mid-sized boats working in the South is the 1999-built *Dreama Klaiber*,

employed by Blessey Marine Services to push oil barges. Although a work boat, the *Dreama Klaiber* has a full guest suite, with double bed, television, microwave, coffee maker, and full bathroom located just below the pilothouse. Beyond that, the comfortably appointed vessel is all business. Forward are big push knees that fit against the barges, and on deck, winches that cinch the connecting cables tight. Aft, and below deck, are two 1,600-hp diesel engines driving 7-foot, 3-inch (2.2m)-diameter propellers through 7:1 gears. This gives the powerful *Dreama Klaiber* and its tow an impressive over-the-water speed of between 6 and 11 mph (9.6 and 17.6kph).

*Right:* The pushboat *M.L. Crochet,* followed by the *Jeanne Marie*, works a chemical barge through the Harvey Locks at Harvey, Louisiana, connecting the Mississippi River with the Harvey Ship Canal.

Sometimes a tug is used to move another tug. On November 10, 1952, when the 203-foot (61.7m) Dutch salvage tug *Swarte Zee* arrived in New York after completing an overseas tow, a New York harbor tug was required to safely berth the larger vessel. The huge, 4200-hp salvage tug sailed with a twenty-five-man crew, but its big single propeller provided little in the way of in-harbor maneuverability.

*Opposite:* Modified to push deep-draft, sea-going barges, this Gulf Fleet tug, its nose cinched into the notch of a petroleum barge, carries a high secondary wheelhouse mounted on tubular columns, as well as a third control house located over the stern winch (which is used during towing operations).

## ARTICULATED TUG/BARGES

Similar in horsepower to the largest of the Mississippi River pushboats are oceangoing tugs specifically designed to push barges at sea as part of an articulated tug/barge (ATB) or integrated tug/barge (ITB) combination. The newer ATB was developed to combine the economics of tugboat and barge operation with the speed and weather reliability of a ship by joining the two units together with an articulating coupling. In the ATB, both the tug and the barge can operate independently, something that is not possible with the earlier developed ITB, which requires dedicated tug/barge units. A number of ITBs are still being used, some with pusher units of up to 11,000 hp, but the concept is waning in favor of the ATB. One of the newest articulated tug/barge combinations employs the 124-foot (37.7m) tug *Nicole Leigh Reinauer* to push the 135,000-barrel-capacity petroleum barge *RTC 135*, both owned by the Reinauer Transportation Company.

To join the *Nicole Leigh Reinauer* and the *RTC 135* together, the nose of the 8,400-hp tug is inserted into a notch at the stern of the barge. On the bows of the tug are twin rams preinstalled in a structural support module. Each ram has a toothed "helmet" at the outboard edge that engages a continuous rack of similar teeth on the barge notch wall. The connection establishes a transverse, fixed horizontal axis about which the tug can pitch independently of the barge in heavy seas and eliminates the need to ballast either vessel in order to bring them to the same height. In addition, it allows the tug to push the barge even when the barge is in a light condition and very high in the water.

*Right*: All tugboat owners wish they had this much access to the machinery spaces of their tugs. Used to sort logs and snag floating debris, the log bronc is a hard worker with "flip-top" access that allows quick maintenance and repair. This unit was made by Chuck Slape of Chuck's Boat and Drive Company, of Longview, Washington, for the U.S. Army Corps of Engineers.

*Opposite, left:* In operation, the log bronc frequently behaves like the bucking bronco after which it is nicknamed. Such a tug requires a skilled operator to safely put it through its paces while maintaining a high degree of productivity.

*Opposite, right:* Hoisted out of the water, the log bronc's well-protected Z-Drive unit and twin skegs are exposed. Besides providing the boat with a sharp turning radius, the skegs contain the engine-water cooling coils and are connected to the drive cage in such a manner that a three-point "foot" is provided on which the boat can be rested when it is taken out of the water.

The *Nicole Leigh Reinauer*, which employs two 11-foot, 6-inch (3.5m)-diameter propellers turning through 5:1 gearing, generates about 75 tons (68t) of forward thrust and is capable of pushing the *RTC 135* at a speed of about 11.5 knots. This compares to a speed of only about 7 knots if the barge had to be towed.

## THE SMALLEST TUGBOATS

If the big Mississippi towboats and the latest ATB tugs are the biggest tugboats engaged in pushing, the smallest are probably the log broncs of the Pacific Northwest. First developed by Fred Nelson, a tugboat operator in Coos Bay, Oregon, the log broncs are miniature tractor tugs that are used to push and position floating logs. They can make up or break down log rafts and help clear floating debris from log ponds and harbors. The broncs are heavily reinforced for their work and are powered by engines of under 250 hp connected to lightweight Z-drives mounted in protective cages. Sawtooth guards are employed along the sides of the hull and at the stem, to "grip" logs for pushing. In addition, a latch-hook is mounted on the stem so a log can be pulled if necessary. Operated much like a bumper car at a carnival, the broncs can quickly sort a high volume of logs in the space of a few hours. The U.S. Navy has also used slightly larger versions of the 15-foot (4.5m) log broncs to move floating pontoons and barges around at the Bremerton Naval Shipyard at Bremerton, Washington.

# WIDENING ROLES

Because of the all-around flexibility of tugboats, they are often called upon to do jobs other than just push and pull. Many have been fitted with pumps and water monitors (also known as cannons) for fire fighting. Some tugs have been called upon to take part in marine salvage by virtue of their towing ability. Others have used their strong hulls for ice breaking. Over the past three decades, two developments within the world's petroleum industry have lead to the creation of two new branches on the tugboat's evolutionary tree. These are the anchor-handling tug and the tanker escort tug. From the latter, a third branch is beginning to develop: the Prevention and Response Tug (PRT). As it becomes more economically beneficial to employ specifically designed vessels to accomplish specific tasks, the roles tugboats play in the maritime world will continue to broaden.

## THE ANCHOR HANDLERS

When the exploration for oil first moved off land and into the waters of the Gulf of Mexico in the early 1950s, conventional tugboats were employed to act as towing and sup-

ply vessels. As the pioneering drilling platforms operated in shallow water, they required only the attention of a traditional tug. When these platforms moved farther offshore, though, they required more specialized handling. By the late 1960s, a new breed of tug was being developed to service and supply these platforms. While the traditional tug profile was retained, the new boats were given a wider and more stable aft working deck, stern-mounted rollers to handle the strain of heavy anchors, and separate steering stations so the master could control the vessel as it worked. When the oil rigs moved into increasingly deeper water, the anchor-handling tugs took on a more rugged profile, adopting raised forecastles protected by heavy rubbing bars. Most were also fitted with hydraulic cranes and many were lengthened to increase their working deck areas. In time, bow thrusters, and even Z-drive propulsion units, were incorporated in the anchor handlers to give them more maneuverability.

The anchor-handling tug has a difficult assignment. Many oil rigs are of the semi-submersible type in that they are floated to their station, then ballasted down

*Left:* A tanker fire is one of the worst disasters that can take place at sea. When the Swedish tanker *Mega Borg* suffered such a calamity in the Gulf of Mexico in 1990, a number of anchor-handling tugs in the area were able to assist in controlling the inferno. Several of these vessels, specifically designed to safeguard offshore oil platforms, have pumping capacities of up to 25,000 gallons (113,650l) per minute.

***Right:*** The nuclear submarine USS *Henry M. Jackson* is assisted into berth at Bangor, Washington, by two military tugs as well as a small utility boat fitted with push knees (two parallel vertical girders attached to the prow of the boat).

***Opposite:*** A modern anchor-handling tug, the 1986-built *Damon Chouest* carries a large hoist at its stern and twin reels mounted forward, above the main deck. The reels carry cables used for the handling and positioning of offshore oil platform anchors. Like most anchor handlers, the *Damon Chouest* has a high-visibility control station facing aft at the pilothouse level and two high-volume water monitors mounted above for fighting fires.

with water to help keep them stable. To make sure they remain in location over the drilling head, they are equipped with numerous anchors. These anchors must be run out and set in position, a task performed by the anchor-handing tugs. When the oil rig needs to be repositioned to another drilling location, the same tugs are called upon to "weigh," or lift, the anchors so they can be retracted by the rig. To accomplish this, the tug backs up and attaches its winch to a pendant cable that runs down to the submerged anchor from a buoy floating on the surface. Once the cable is attached, the winch places tension on the line, then natural wave action on the tug's hull is used to "luff" the anchor out of the mud. Once the anchor is free of the bottom, the tug keeps it suspended on the cable while the rig reels it in. In some cases, the anchor is fully raised and landed on the tug's deck, either for repair or for the attachment of "piggyback" anchors (added to provide more grip). The anchor is then reset on the sea floor in the same manner that it is brought in.

One of North America's most modern anchor-handling tugs is the *Atlantic Eagle*, built by Canada's Irving Shipbuilding Group at Halifax, Nova Scotia, and operated by Saint John–based Atlantic Towing. Illustrating the loads these tugs must handle, the vessel's 8-foot, 10-inch (2.7m) diameter stern roller has a safe working load (SWL) of 440 metric tons (485t), while the winches used to handle the anchors have brake-holding load capacities of 430 metric tons (474t) and are equipped with steel cables 3 inches (7.6cm) thick. The tug's working deck provides a clear area of 1,825 square feet (167.9m2) and can support a load of 1,100 metric tons (1, 212.5t). Two 7,200-hp diesel engines are used to drive controllable-pitch propellers housed in Kort nozzles. This provides a bollard pull of 165 metric tons (181.9t), yet gives the vessel a light running speed of 16 knots. Because of the degree of maneuverability required while working in close proximity to an oil platform, the 246-foot (74.8m) vessel has been equipped with three 1,200-hp thruster units, one located aft and two forward. All of these can be controlled from a single joystick in the wheelhouse, keeping the big tug perfectly positioned over its work.

## ESCORT TUGS

While anchor-handling tugs have been specifically developed to serve the needs of offshore oil platforms, modern escort tugs owe their existence to the proliferation of gigantic petroleum tankers.

In the early 1980s, new regulations came into effect in Washington State calling for tankers to be escorted by tugboats in case the large ships lost steering or engine power. When the U.S. tanker *Exxon Valdez* grounded off Alaska in 1989, causing a massive oil spill in Prince William Sound, federal regulations were enacted calling for the "best available technology" to be employed in all tanker escort work. The U.S. Coast Guard studied the use of conventional shafted-propeller tugs for this work and concluded that they were not suitable for handling large tankers at speeds in excess of 3 knots. In addition, the agency found that operating a conventional tug forward of such a tanker using a towline was "extremely dangerous," as was operating aft on a long hawser if the tanker's speed was greater than 6 knots.

*Opposite:* With its Voith Schneider propulsion unit mounted forward, the Crowley tug *Guide* operates stern first as it assists in moving a large container ship through Los Angeles harbor.

The U.S Coast Guard's *Hawser* is a light tugboat designed to both assist ships and break ice in protected harbors.

***Opposite:*** Crowley Maritime's large escort tug *Tan'erliq*, its propulsion units mounted forward, has been specially designed to accompany laden petroleum tankers out of Alaska's Prince William Sound.

Tractor-style tugs, with their thrusters placed at one end and towing point and fendering at the other, are considered better suited for escort work because their configuration essentially eliminates the possibility of "girding" or "broaching," during which the tug is pulled sideways by the bigger ship and possibly capsized. Likewise, the agile tractors can more easily avoid a "stemming" situation, in which the tug is pressed up against the bow of the vessel being assisted. Although the Coast Guard imposed no specific regulations concerning tug type or design at the time of its study, it noted that

Washington State's escort regulations called for tugs to have installed propulsion power numerically equal to 5 percent of the escorted tanker's DWT (the amount, in tons, the tanker could carry). This would mean a tug of about 6,000 hp would be needed to escort a tanker of about 120,000 DWT.

By the time of the study, Foss Maritime of Seattle had considerable experience using its early Voith Schneider–propelled tugs in escort work. With a preferential-usage contract signed with tanker owners BP Oil Shipping Company and ARCO Marine Inc., Foss decided to build two larger tugs that would be specifically designed to

brake and control large tankers. In addition, these new tugs would be capable of berthing and unberthing tankers, and if necessary, fighting fires. In order to control the mass of a loaded oil tanker entering port, the escort tugs were to be used like "large remote active rudders" to help steer and stop the vessel. To accomplish this procedure, they would take a line off the stern of the tanker while it was still moving at approximately 10 knots and then swing out and turn their hull against the direction the tanker was moving. To use a normal tugboat in this manner would risk an immediate capsizing, but the new tugs were to be powered by the proven Voith Schneider cycloidal propulsion units. Because the angle of the twirling blades under the escort tug's hull can be adjusted to control their degree of bite into the water, the tug can quickly shift in response to the pull of the tanker. In early 1994, the two Foss "enhanced tractor tugs," the *Lindsey Foss* and *Garth Foss*, were delivered, each of 8,000 hp.

## 8000-hp ESCORT TUGS

At the time of their debut, the 155-foot-by-46-foot (45.6 by 14m) *Lindsey Foss* and *Garth Foss* were the largest cycloidal propulsion tugs in the world. The five blades within their Voith Schneider systems stand 7 feet, 5 inches (2.2m) high and turn at a speed of 66 rpm. At the stern of each vessel is a large fixed rudder, or "skeg," that measures 340 square feet (31.3m$^2$) in surface area. The skeg enhances the tug's ability to steer and stop a moving ship. For safety, the new escort tugs were equipped with a "transom link," developed by Foss, which consists of a titanium-alloy hook light enough in weight that it can be deployed and attached to the "tag line" of a tanker by a

***Opposite:*** Swinging in stern-first to take a line off the tanker *Denali*, the escort tug *Nanuo* takes up a standard escorting stance off Alaska. Once the line is secured, the tug can easily control the larger ship by shearing off to port or starboard while using its deep hull skeg and propulsion units to act as both a brake and remote rudder.

*Opposite:* One of 21
Dorchester Heights–class tugs completed by Orange Shipbuilding
Company of Orange, Texas, for the
U.S. Army, the stoutly built *ST-903*
can be lifted on and off ship for
overseas transport.

single deckhand. During a demonstration of the effectiveness of the *Lindsey Foss* and its transom link, it took only 80 seconds for the escort tug to spin around, make the emergency towline connection, and be in position to halt a 90,000-dwt tanker that was moving along as if it had lost power.

Since the adoption of the large Foss tanker escort tugs in Puget Sound, even stronger tanker escort tugs capable of more than 10,000 hp have been built for operation in Alaska's Prince William Sound by Crowley Maritime. However, instead of meeting an arriving tanker, as is the case in Puget Sound, these tugs escort departing tankers. They remain tethered to a tanker at its stern, using a special synthetic line, for a distance of 28 miles (44.8m), with a second escort tug running alongside. It was in Prince William Sound that the tanker *Exxon Valdez* was navigating outbound when it ran onto rocks in 1989. Such Crowley escort tugs as the *Nanuq* and *Tan'erliq* are designed to control and halt tankers the same way the *Lindsey Foss* and *Garth Foss* do. They shear off at an angle to the tow load and use their deep hull skegs, in combination with their cycloidal propellers, to produce steering and stopping forces greatly in excess of their static bollard pull.

## PREVENTION AND RESPONSE

The high-powered escort tugs of Prince William Sound are now being joined by yet another specialized vessel, the Prevention and Response Tug. These tugs are also 10,000 hp, but utilize Z-drive propulsion instead of cycloidal propulsion. Although they are not considered as maneuverable as the cycloidal drive tractors, which are required to

pace and control a tanker at speeds of more than 10 knots, the PRTs have more direct bollard pull. This comes into play in deep water situations where a tanker may have to be towed rather than stopped. The PRTs have also been designed to meet spill prevention and response requirements at the petroleum-loading terminal at Valdez and can function in a ship-assist and -escort capacity when needed. Each PRT carries two oil spill recovery skiffs on board and a substantial amount of deployable spill control boom (a long floating containment line put out to keep floating oil in one location). Below deck, the 140-foot (42.5m) tugs have a tank large enough to store up to 43,000 gallons (162,755l) of recovered oil.

## COMMERCIAL TUGS FOR U.S. NAVY SHIPS

The U.S. military has not been building as many tugboats as it once did, and the navy is now replacing many of its older Yard Tug Boats (YTBs) with modern vessels contracted from private ship-assist firms. Because of this, Moran Towing has accepted its first Z-drive tractor tugs from Washburn & Doughty Associates of Maine for U.S. Navy work in Virginia. The 92-foot (27.9m) tractors are distinct from the long line of conventional tugboats Moran has operated through the years. Besides their modern propulsion, the 4200-hp "Azimuthing Stern Drive" (ASD) tugs have been specifically built to meet navy requirements. For firefighting, they carry two monitors located at the forward starboard and port quarters of the pilothouse to provide a full 360 degrees of coverage. These monitors are fed by high-capacity pumps with a discharge rate of 3,000

gallons (11,355l) per minute each. The tractor tugs have also been provided with extra seating in their day room areas to accommodate navy crews being ferried to and from their vessels. For submarine work, the Moran tractors have been equipped with full underwater fendering at the stem and along the sides.

## COMPACT ARMY TUGS

While the navy is turning over much of its tugboat work to private industry, the U.S. Army has taken delivery of a new type of compact harbor tug that has been specifically designed to be loaded aboard a larger ship and freighted overseas. Known as the Dorchester Heights class, the 1280-hp, twin screw tugs are only 59 feet (17.9m) long and 22 feet (6.7m) wide but are stoutly built. By using eyelets welded onto the decks, they can be hoisted aboard military transport ships, secured on special cradles, and transported to any area of the world. Once at their destination, they can be lowered into the water and put to work immediately. Duties include berthing ships, pushing barges, and towing landing pontoons. All the tugs can be armed and are fitted with push knees and towing winches. A special "black box" mounted in the pilothouse of these little tugs informs other U.S. forces electronically that they are "friendly" vessels.

# DESIGN, BUILD, AND LAUNCH

When building a modern tugboat, the design and construction are handled in much the same way that they are when a house is built, except that the tug must be built for motion. A prospective owner identifies what specifications he needs and contracts with an architect to help create the best solution. Owner and architect work hand-in-hand to make sure the final product responds to the original demand yet is built as economically and quickly as possible. To construct a tugboat, a naval architect will examine the most efficient hull shape to use and the best propulsion machinery to employ. The architect will also insure the tug meets all stability requirements and can pass inspection for operating certificates and insurance. A third party in this process is the shipbuilder chosen to build the tug, although some owners will build their own tugs (and some shipyards provide their own architects).

## TUGBOAT DESIGN ELEMENTS

When the job description of the new tug has been firmly established and a conceptual design worked out, the owner, architect, and shipyard begin drawing on previous experience to come up with the best possible vessel. Former tug designs may be used, but they will most likely be upgraded to take into account feedback received from customers and crew. Good visibility is a known requirement for safe ship handling, and modern ship-assist tugs are being given 360 degrees of viewing range from the pilothouse. This is accomplished by providing more window area and by routing engine exhaust through narrow stacks rather than broad funnels. To reduce sun glare, pilothouse windows are tilted inwards at the bottom, and to make sure the captain can see above, smaller windows

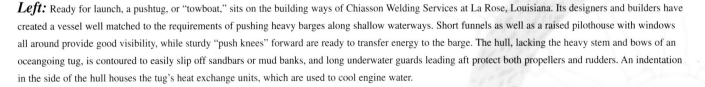

*Left:* Ready for launch, a pushtug, or "towboat," sits on the building ways of Chiasson Welding Services at La Rose, Louisiana. Its designers and builders have created a vessel well matched to the requirements of pushing heavy barges along shallow waterways. Short funnels as well as a raised pilothouse with windows all around provide good visibility, while sturdy "push knees" forward are ready to transfer energy to the barge. The hull, lacking the heavy stem and bows of an oceangoing tug, is contoured to easily slip off sandbars or mud banks, and long underwater guards leading aft protect both propellers and rudders. An indentation in the side of the hull houses the tug's heat exchange units, which are used to cool engine water.

*Right:* Workers at Bollinger Shipyards of Lockport, Louisiana, assemble on the wharf to watch as the hull of the tug *Vera Bisso* is launched into the water, upside down and sideways. The hull had been previously completed in a nearby assembly hall where ducted propellers, shafts, rudders, and a protective keel skeg had been fitted.

*Opposite:* Airtight, the hull will float upside down until attending tugs push it into position to be flipped upright by a mobile crane. The engines and other equipment will then be installed and the super-structure and pilothouse attached. "Lines" seen on the bottom of the hull represent the tug's keel cooling system, where engine water, running through long pipes, is cooled by river water.

are cut in the pilothouse roof. In some situations, where the tug's working decks might be obstructed from the pilothouse, remote TV cameras are employed. Fore and aft control stations are also becoming popular as modern tugs increasingly work with both their stem and stern.

To determine the right hull design and propulsion plant combination for a tugboat, the naval architect must balance cost to benefit. Power plants may be chosen on a basis of

horsepower-to-size or on what type of financing package the equipment supplier is willing to provide. Future repair and maintenance requirements must also be figured in to the initial design. Stern-mounted Z-drives have become more popular because they are better protected under the rear of a boat and more accessible for repair and replacement. The stern positioning also results in a shallower draft vessel, an advantage for operators who work in limited water depths or

who would face additional expense if forced to dry-dock a tug with deeply projecting propulsion units.

Because modern commercial ships are built with thinner steel hull plating than in former years, modern ship-assist tugs are usually given a rounder nose to spread their pushing force across the 8-foot (2.4m) spacing between the larger vessel's vertical internal supports. To avoid damage from the bigger ship's heavily projecting bows, tug pilothouses are

set farther back on the hull and carry retractable or foldable light masts and antennas. If the tug is being built specifically for ship-assist work, the pitch of its propeller may be set to provide maximum thrust at around 2 knots. If the tug is slated for long-distance towing, the blades are more likely pitched for maximum power at around 7 knots. Gearing will be chosen to match the engine's horsepower/rpm curve with the size and pitch of the propeller used to suit the tug's expected employment.

*Right:* This schematic diagram provides a good idea of the fore-thought that goes into the design and construction of a modern tug. Designed as the pusher unit for an Articulated Tug/Barge combination by Ocean Tug & Barge Engineering Corporation (of Milford, Massachusetts), the *S/R Everett* is one of the largest and most power-ful tugboats ever built. It was con-structed by J.M. Martinac Shipbuilding (of Tacoma, Washington) and incorporates a toothed "helmet" (seen on the side of the hull under the wheelhouse) that engages a continuous rack of similar teeth on the notch wall of the barge it will push. In this man-ner, a transverse, fixed horizontal axis is established about which the tug can pitch independently of the barge in heavy seas and in all load conditions.

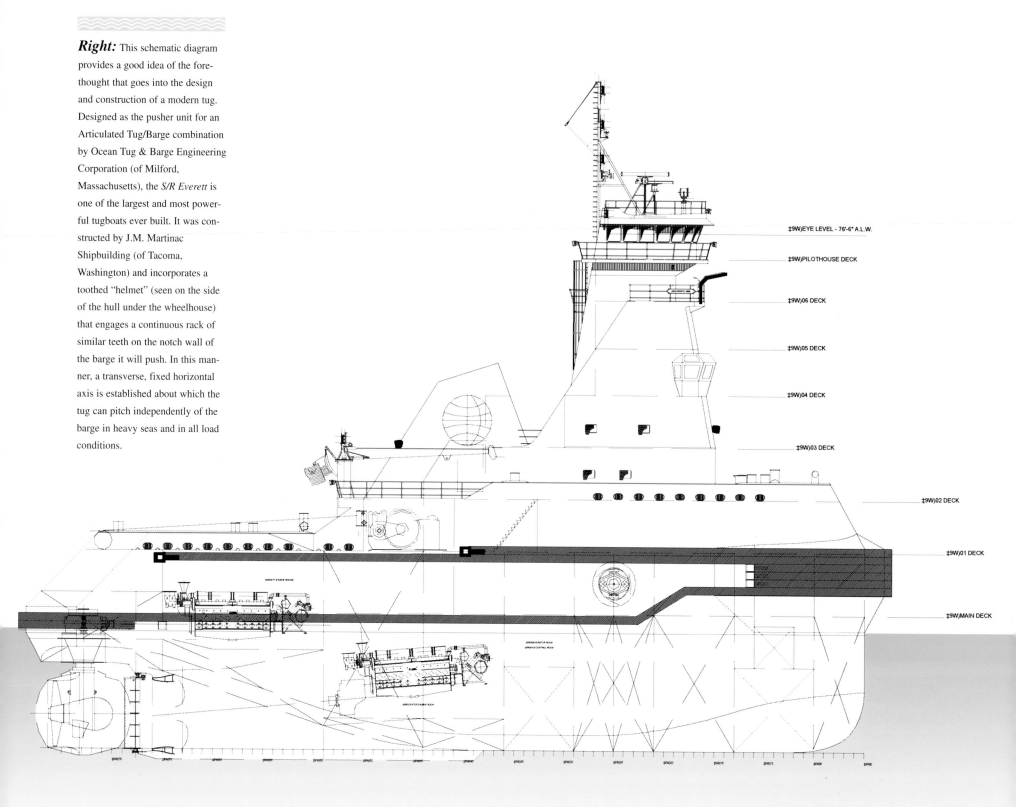

## CREW SAFETY AND COMFORT

Equipment and systems on the tugboat are chosen to meet the job requirements as well as specific operational regulations. Deck winches may be selected to handle steel cable or synthetic rope. In most cases, they are controlled directly from the pilothouse. This is a safety factor that eliminates the need for any of the tug's crew to be near moving machinery. Environmental regulations, both state and federal, may require the tug to have a holding tank for sewage and an overflow tank for fuel, as well as a reinforced hull around the engine room area. Because of heat buildup, tugs working in the South may have the power supplies for their radios and radar arrays mounted under the pilothouse rather than inside it. Similarly, tugs designed for operation in

***Above:*** Designed to feed a crew of eight, the galley of the *S/R Everett* is located on the upper decks, away from engine noise, and features all the modern conveniences, including stainless steel fixtures, an industrial oven, a dishwasher, and plenty of storage space.

***Left:*** Functioning as the propulsion unit of a 140,000-barrel capacity "tanker," the *S/R Everett* houses unusually large engines in the shape of two EMD 16-710G General Motors diesels, each developing 3,600 hp.

**Right:** Two tugs, attached by cable and working in line, prepare to pull a newly built, 60 foot (18.2m)–by–24 foot (7.3m) towboat off its building ways at La Rose, Louisiana. Once in the water, the new boat will be berthed alongside a fitting-out pier for the installation of final equipment and painting.

**Opposite, top:** Shipyard workers at Fashion Blacksmith, in Crescent City, California, complete the installation of new 74-inch (1.9m) propeller nozzles on Weststar Marine Services' 71-foot (21.6m) tugboat *Solana*. The modification, which includes the installation of new flanking rudders forward of the propellers, reduces steerage somewhat compared to open propellers but increases speed by about 1 knot and bollard pull by 30 percent.

**Opposite, bottom:** One of two 3,800-hp Caterpillar 3612 marine diesel engines installed in the 180 foot (54.7m)–by–48 foot (14.6m) towboat *John Paul Eckstein*, built by Quality Shipyards at Houma, Louisiana, for Marquette Transportation of Paducah, Kentucky.

northern latitudes are fitted out with special heating coils to keep ice off decks and ladders. Noise is a constant concern for tugboat crews, so most vessels are being built with additional soundproofing in the pilothouse and accommodation areas. Although all of these details add to the cost of the tug, the savings gained in insurance and in the well being of the crew are impossible to overestimate.

## BUILDING A TUG

When the tugboat's hull and propulsion arrangement have been selected and mechanical fixtures chosen, the tug's design moves beyond the conceptual drawing to a full set of engineering plans. In today's high-tech environment, this will most likely be performed using a computer-aided design and engineering program. These programs check for errors and insure components will fit properly, then transmit the specific cutting and bending instructions for each steel plate and section of pipe to the fabricating machinery. This machinery may be located within the shipyard or at a distant plant, but the materials are scheduled to arrive on site as required. Hulls are usually built upside down, then rotated right side up, either on land or in the water, after which the superstructure and fixtures are added. In this manner, a small shipyard can build a fairly large and complicated tugboat in a relatively short amount of time.

## NEW TUGS FROM OLD

Not all tugboat operators elect to build a new vessel to meet changing requirements. Like homeowners, they may chose to update or build an addition. Over the past several years, Foss Maritime has changed the propulsion systems of several of its older tugs to give them more power and flexibility. In one series of ship-assist tugboats, the conventional twin-propeller drive was removed and replaced by twin stern-mounted Z-drive units along with higher horsepower engines. To accommodate the 360-degree swing of the Z-drives, as well as to insure good water flow through the ducted propellers, the hulls of the tugs had to be substantially modified. This required a new bottom contour aft and a new keel profile. Topside, a line winch was installed forward of the pilothouse, while the pilothouse itself was completely rebuilt and moved back several feet. The modifications resulted in a modern, high-performance ship-handling tug with a substantially increased bollard pull at half the cost of a newly built tug.

# CHAPTER SIX

# OUT TO PASTURE

The sturdy construction of tugboats has allowed a good many to remain afloat long after their days of commercial employment have ended. A few have been preserved as museum pieces, and fewer still have been kept operational (some with their original powerplants). Others have ended up as private yachts, floating motels, or live-aboard homes. Several have been pulled ashore for exhibit, either in whole or in part. Most have simply rotted away and exist now only in photographs.

One such casualty is the *Seguin* of 1884, a tug famous in the New England area that had to be dismantled in 1988 because of her deteriorated condition. Another is the wooden-hulled *John Taxis*, built in Chester, Pennsylvania, in 1869 as the *William Stewart* and once considered North America's oldest tugboat; it was demolished in the 1990s at Wilmington, North Carolina, when its hull was found to be too deteriorated to restore. At Gold Beach, Oregon, the remains of the 1881-built *Mary D. Hume* are sinking into the mud after the tug slipped off its supporting cradle in 1985.

## MUSEUM TUGS

Museums have proven particularly fond of tugboats because the vessels are small enough to easily display and serve as a good example of a working ship. The older wooden-hulled tugs are difficult to care for but several remain afloat, maintained either by museums, preservation societies, or private parties. A beautiful wooden-hulled tug, the steam-powered *Master*, is located at the Vancouver Maritime Museum in Vancouver, British Columbia. Built in 1922, the 72-foot (21.9m) *Master* is one of the last wooden-hulled steam-powered tugs still capable of operating. On rare occasions, it can be seen in close proximity to another operational wooden-hulled tugboat, the 1889-built *Arthur Foss*, which is based at the Northwest Seaport in Seattle, Washington. A third wooden-hulled tug that is still operational is the 1930-built *W.O. Decker*, found at the South Street Seaport in New York City. This little tug, originally steam powered but now dieselized, is also one of the few tugs that can occasionally be seen working up against the side of a square-rigged sailing ship.

*Left:* Lit up like a Christmas tree, and with fendering still slung over its side, the 1924-built *New York Central No. 16* functions today as part of a seafood restaurant located near the Cape Cod Canal, Massachusetts.

*Right:* On display at the H. Lee White Museum at Oswego, New York, this U.S. Army LT-5 tug participated in D-Day landings during World War II as the *Major Elisha K. Henson*, later serving the U.S. Army Corps of Engineers as the *John F. Nash*. Principally used for towing, the military tug has been fitted with a low-slung stem fender for barge and scow work.

*Opposite:* The World War II Navy tugboat *Hoga* (YT-146), with some of its crew's laundry drying on the upper deck, assists the USS *Montgomery* (DM-17) away from the pier at Pearl Harbor, Hawaii, on May 10, 1943. Today, the sixty-year-old tug is the focus of a restoration project being promoted by the USS *Hoga* YT-146 Association of Florida.

Coal-fired steam tugboats are becoming harder to find, but the *Baltimore*, on Chesapeake Bay, is still capable of firing up its boiler and turning out a good cloud of smoke. Likewise, San Francisco's oceangoing steam-powered tug, *Hercules*, remains operational, although fired by oil rather than coal. The nearby *Eppleton Hall* no longer operates, but it remains unique among North American–preserved tugs because of its twin paddlewheel arrangement and twin side-lever "Grasshopper" steam engines. A paddlewheel tug still capable of getting up a good head of steam is the sternwheeler *Portland*, berthed on the Willamette River at Portland, Oregon. This shallow-draft river tug, the final sternwheel ship-assist vessel to work in a major North American port, is the last of her breed, yet competes annually in river races.

The *Edna G* (built in 1896), a Great Lakes "winding" tug that at one time assisted ore carriers to their berths, is on display at Two Harbors, Minnesota. Before its retirement in 1981, the *Edna G* was the last coal-fired steam-powered tug in commercial operation in North

America. Its original fore-and-aft compound condesing engine was never replaced.

Diesel-powered tugs are not given the same respect as steamers, but their lines remain classical and many were originally powered by steam. The *Jupiter* of Philadelphia, which gave up its steam power plant after World War II but remains active using diesel, is an early example. Another preserved tug, originally and still a diesel, is the 44-foot (13.4m) *Kingston II*, completed by Electric Boat in 1937 and maintained by Mystic Seaport in Mystic, Connecticut. The *Kingston II* was one of the very first all-welded vessels built in the United States and is powered by an early General Motors diesel. A wartime survivor is the 114-foot (34.6m) *John F. Nash*, which took part in the D-Day land-

ings at Normandy under the name *Major Elisha K. Henson*. Built in 1943, the tug is berthed at the H. Lee White Museum at Oswego, New York, and is considered the last essentially unmodified example of a military Large Harbor Tug (LT). It is also the only known surviving U.S. Army vessel associated with the D-Day landings.

Another historic World War II tug is the 100-foot (30.4m) *Hoga*, laid up within the San Francisco Bay mothball fleet and awaiting restoration. Built for the U.S. Navy in 1940, the *Hoga* was stationed at Pearl Harbor when the Japanese air attack took place in 1941 and managed to assist several damaged vessels, including the battleship USS *Nevada*. It is the last surviving navy vessel from the attack still afloat.

*Opposite:* The last of her type ever built, the sternwheel tug *Portland,* once owned by the Port of Portland, remains operational in Portland, Oregon, under the care of the Oregon Maritime Center & Museum.

*Above:* An operating exhibit at the South Street Seaport in New York City, the wooden-hulled tug *W.O. Decker* is sometimes used to move sailing ships berthed at the port.

***Above:*** A frequent participant in Pacific Northwest tugboat gatherings, the Canadian tug *Master*, completed in 1922, is one of the last steam-propelled, wooden-hulled tugboats still remaining in operating condition.

***Opposite:*** Carrying the elongated lower deckhouse of a harbor inspection vessel, the tug *Baltimore* rests at Baltimore, Maryland, where it is maintained by the Baltimore Museum of Industry. During the winter months, covers are placed on the tug's funnel and forward windows for protection.

## TUG RESTORATION

The restoration of a tugboat is a time-consuming and expensive process, but several are being brought back to life. One is the 98-foot (29.8m) wooden hulled *Luna*, completed in 1930 as the first diesel-electric tugboat built for a commercial tugboat company in the United States. After sinking at its dock in 1990, it is currently being rebuilt in Boston, Massachusetts, by the *Luna* Preservation Society. Another wooden-hulled tug being restored following submersion is the *Sand Man*, built in 1908 as one of the first gasoline-powered tugboats on the Pacific Coast. Its original heavy-duty gas engine was displayed at Seattle's Alaska-Yukon-Pacific Exposition in 1909. *The Sand Man* is under reconstruction funded by the *Sand Man* Foundation of Olympia, Washington.

## ON DRY LAND

Because of the difficulty and expense of maintaining older vessels afloat, a number of vintage tugboats have been pulled up on dry land. At Coos Bay, Oregon, the tugboat *Koos No. 2,* built at Marshfield, Oregon, in 1924 for Knutson Towboat, is now part of an extensive marine interpretive center. Visitors to the center can easily see the underwater lines of the wooden-hulled tug and step around

*Right:* Moored along the shores of Harriet Island, across the Mississippi River from St. Paul, Minnesota, the Covington Inn is actually a salvaged towboat that was transformed into an elegant bed and breakfast. Built in 1946, the 300-ton *Covington* plied the waters of the Mississippi and Ohio rivers for decades, pushing barges loaded with liquid cargo (note the prominent push knees). In 1993, she was lying neglected in a salvage yard in Louisiana, where she was found and then restored by the River Valley Preservation Company, which brought her to St. Paul.

*Left:* The Pilot House Suite is a two-story accommodation that extends from the second to the third deck of the Covington Inn and (as was necessary in its original incarnation) commands the best view. Note the original brass controls in front of the windows.

*Below:* The Master's Quarters is one of the most spacious rooms at the Covington Inn, with a view upstream and access to the seventy-foot (21.3m) second deck.

*Pages 108–109:* A stranger afloat in American waters, the British-built *Eppleton Hall* is representative of the earliest of the side-paddle steam tugs that first entered service in northern England during the 1810s and 1820s. The 1914-built tug was purchased by private interests in 1969 and brought to the United States under its own power. It was donated to the National Park Service in 1979.

*Right:* Once America's oldest extant tugboat, the *John Taxis*, shown here afloat at Wilmington, North Carolina, in 1982, had to be demolished several years ago because of its deteriorating condition.

to the stern to view the three-bladed bronze propeller. The *Koos No. 2* was retired from the the Knutson fleet in 1987 and donated to the community of Coos Bay for exhibition.

Another old tug on dry land is the *Mathilda* (1899), displayed at the Hudson River Maritime Center at Kingston, New York. Although built in Canada for service at Montreal, the steel-hulled *Mathilda* is representative of the early river tugs that worked the Hudson and the smaller tugs that worked New York Harbor. Another former New York tug now high and dry is the *Dorothy* of 1890, the first vessel built by Newport News Shipbuilding and Drydock, now the United States' largest shipbuilder. Salvaged in the mid-1970s, the iron-hulled tug sits on a concrete and steel pad in front of the company's administrative offices at Newport News, Virginia.

Not all preserved tugboats are found near the water. At the Miracle of America Museum in Polson, Montana, sits the 65-foot (19.7m) *Paul Bunyan*, once used as a logging tug on Flathead Lake. The tugboat was rescued by the museum in 1987 and trucked 35 miles (56km) overland to be restored as an exhibit. Nor is this the only tugboat to have been incorporated into land-based structures to add a bit of nautical atmosphere. One of the former Moran tugboats, the *Richard J. Moran*, was pulled ashore at Boothbay, Maine, some years ago and is now part of a motel aptly named the "Tugboat Inn." In a similar vein, the 112-foot (34m) *John Wanamaker*, built in 1924 for the city of Philadelphia and the last operating coastal steam screw tug in North America, serves as a restaurant at Camden, Maine. One of the New York Central's famous car float

*Above:* Ocean tides are slowly reclaiming the remains of the 1881-built Pacific Coast tugboat *Mary D. Hume* at Gold Beach, Oregon. The historic tug collapsed the wooden cradles it was being set on in 1985 and settled into the mud at its present location. Partially submerged each day, the lower portion of the tug is home to a thriving community of algae.

tugs, the 1924-built *New York Central No. 16*, can be seen near Cape Cod Canal, Massachusetts, where its upper half forms part of a restaurant. A much smaller tug, the 27-foot (8.2m) *Irene*, is on a trailer at Coos Bay, Oregon, but city officials hope to one day display it in a giant bottle made of plastic.

## RETIRED TUGBOAT ASSOCIATION

Members of the International Retired Tugboat Association are not yet willing to have their vessels mounted in bottles. Many of these enthusiasts own and operate their own tugs, a number of which are still employed in limited commercial service. Although most of the tugboats are small in size, several have interesting stories to tell.

### THE DODO BIRD

The 37-foot (11.2m) tug *Annie*, owned by Forbes and Ann Jones of LaConner, Washington, is a case in point. The tugboat was built in the beginning of the twentieth century by a man who took ten years to complete it, using a boiler, propeller, and steam engine salvaged from a local wrecking yard. He then fitted the boat out using a steam pump, valves, piping, and miscellaneous fittings taken from an 1875-built tug, the *Hector*, which he found abandoned and burning on the beach one night. After his tug was finished, in 1934, the builder was required to document it with local authorities. At a loss for a name, he said his boat was "just an old Dodo Bird," and the boat was officially recorded as the *Dodo*. The *Dodo* operated for more than four decades using its original wood and coal-fired "Wards" boiler, but was refitted in 1977 with a newer boiler acquired from a tourist launch at Disney World. Although the modern boiler performed

_Below:_ Once mounted at the
end of the Cunard Line passenger
pier in New York City, the 1899-
built _Mathilda_ has since been
moved to the Hudson River
Maritime Center, located at
Kingston, New York, for display.

admirably, burning just 3.5 gallons (13.2l) of fuel per hour, it was eventually replaced, and today the _Annie_, as the _Dodo_ is now known, is diesel-powered.

## THE VERY FIRST DIESEL TUG

Diesel-powered right from the start, the 70-foot (21.3m) _Chickamauga_ is now used as a live-aboard tugboat by Eric Davis of Seattle, Washington. Built in 1915 for $7,700, the _Chickamauga_ was the first full-powered diesel tug in North America, and one of the first on the West Coast to be fitted with towing machinery. Designed by L.E. Geary, the hull

was built of Washington State Douglas fir using 10-inch (25.4cm) frames and 2.75-inch (7cm) fir planking, except for pine stop-waters (small "dams" located forward of the pilothouse that deflect water coming over the bow), an oak stern, and sheathing of iron bark. The boat has gone through its original engine, as well as three others, and today is propelled by a 510-hp General Motors engine.

## FOSS VETERAN

A tug originally coal-fired but now diesel-propelled is the 63-foot (19.1m) _Elf_, built in 1902 for Tacoma Tug Boat

Company. This little tug, along with two others, helped forge the foundation of Foss Maritime's tugboating interests during World War I. Foss purchased the *Elf* for work in Puget Sound and renamed it *Foss No. 15.* Just before World War II, it was converted to diesel. The U.S. Army then put it to work towing barges between Puget Sound and Alaska when conventional cargo ships became scarce. Although started as a stopgap measure, the tug and barge trade to Alaska remains one of the world's busiest long-haul towing operations. After the war, the *Foss No. 15* worked in the Foss fleet until 1970, when it was retired with more than a half century's service. Today, restored, re-engined, and rechristened with its original name, the *Elf* is operated by Earl Van Diest of Port Orchard, Washington.

### CANADIAN BUILT

Not all old tugs pass to new owners with a clearly documented history. When Ron and Nancy Drinkwater purchased the 30-foot (9.1m) tugboat *Aix* in 1982, the boat was in very poor shape and held few clues as to its past.

However, as the couple restored their tug they also researched local archives. Although it took some time, they found a Captain H.J. Anderson had built the tug on Canada's Skeena River in 1908, originally for the towing of fishing dories to the mouth of the river. In 1916, the boat was purchased by new owners, and in 1920 underwent a major rebuilding during which it gained 10 feet (3m) in length and a new steam engine. The tugboat was then used to tow brick barges before being demoted to a logging crew vessel in the 1950s. Today, renamed the *Nan Lea*, the vessel has been re-registered under its original number and is powered by a 57-hp Ford Tunney Queen Diesel.

### TUG HOME

Converting an old tugboat into a comfortable home takes a great deal of work. The 75-foot (22.8m) tug *Sally S,* acquired by Greg and Betty Mallory of Seattle, Washington, in 1996, is a good example. Built in 1927, the sixty-nine-year-old tug required a complete makeover to function as a live-aboard residence. Among other things,

***Above:*** Lying in the weeds along the bank of the Snake River near Lewiston, Idaho, the towboat *Jean* is considered unique among Pacific Northwest river tugboats in that it was built as a steel-hulled sternwheeler with dual sternwheels, each powered by a separate steam engine. This made the *Jean* a "tractor tug" of her day, able to spin with exceptional maneuverability. The 168-foot (51.1m) vessel was completed by Commercial Iron Works at Portland, Oregon, in 1938 and spent nearly four decades towing log barges for Crown Zellerbach. Retired in 1957, the boat was converted into a floating machine shop following the removal of her engines and boilers. In 1979 ownership passed to the Idaho Historical Society, and in 1989 it was listed on the National Register of Historic Places.

**Right:** Tugboating for the fun of it! Members of the International Retired Tugboat Association race their boats past the Seattle waterfront during the annual Seattle Tugboat Races, held each May. Founded in 1972 with thirteen members and three tugs, the association has since grown to include more than 300 members and 120 tugs. The tug *Raccoon* (seen here), owned and skippered by Lawrence Graves, was one of the associations' three original tugboats.

this included new equipment such as toilets ("heads") and sewage holding tanks; plumbing; galley; cabinets; sink; refrigerator; stove; wiring; generator; battery banks; and a hot-water heating system throughout the hull and the engine room. Topside, the pilothouse was completely remodeled and new navigational equipment and electronics were installed. In addition, the overhead on both the pilothouse and the main cabin had to be replaced. Outside, the entire foredeck—including deck, deck beams, knees, and shelves—required replacement, as did some of the deck structuring and fendering. Fortunately for the Mallorys' pocketbook, when the *Sally S* was drydocked, its bottom was found to be in sound condition. It is now berthed among the working tugs of the Fremont Tug company fleet on Seattle's Lake Union.

## BUNK & BREAKFAST

For those adventurous souls who might like to try a night on a tug before owning one, the tugboat *Challenger* operates as a "bunk & breakfast" on Seattle's Lake Union. A 96-foot (29.2m) wartime TP-class U.S. Army tug, *Challenger* was for many years operated for British Columbia's Island Tug & Barge as the *Challenger*, later becoming the *Seaspan Challenger*. Although the deckhouse has been extended aft and a number of other modifications have been made (mostly in the interest of increased space and comfort), the tug remains a good example of the many series-built tugs that were turned out during World War II. *Challenger* is also one of the few classes of tugs built to carry freight, and once supported an aft cargo hold—now a guest lounge—capable of storing 75 tons (68t).

## Tugboat Associations

International Retired Tugboat Association
1030 W. Nickerson #6
Seattle, WA 98119-1449
Dues: $13 (US)/$15 (Canadian) per year for
*Tug's Wake*, published three times a year

Tugboat Enthusiasts Society of America
420 49th Street E., Lot 127
Palmetto, FL 34221
Dues: $30 per year for *TugBitts,* published
four times a year

## Websites

www.covingtoninn.com/index2.htm
The website for the Covington Inn, located
off Harriet Island in St. Paul, Minnesota, a
floating bed and breakfast on the
Mississippi River

home.pacifier.com/~rboggs/index.html
The Tugpage on the Merchant Marine &
Maritime website features stories and pho-
tographs of several historic tugboats

www.nps.gov/safr/local/eppie.html
The homepage for the San Francisco
Maritime National Historical Park, home
dock of the *Eppleton Hall* and *Hercules* as
well as many other vessels

www.tugboats.com/index.html
The homepage of a terrific general-interest
website for tugboat enthusiasts of every
stripe, including modelers and historians

# BIBLIOGRAPHY

## Periodicals

*The Compass*, var. ed. Brooklyn, New York:
Mobile International Aviation and Marine
Sales, Inc. (quarterly company publication)
*Harbour & Shipping Journal*, var. ed. West
Vancouver, British Columbia, Canada:
Progress Publishing Co. Ltd. (monthly
from British Columbia)
*International Tug & Salvage*. Surrey, United
Kingdom: International Tug and Salvage
(semi-monthly publication from the U.K.)
*Marine News*. Kent, United Kingdom: The
World Ship Society (monthly journal of the
World Ship Society)
*Nautical Gazette*, var. ed. New York, New
York (old maritime paper)
*The Pacific Maritime Magazine*. Seattle,
Washington: Pacific Maritime Magazine
(monthly)
*Steamboat Bill*. Providence, Rhode Island:
Steamship Historical Society of America
(quarterly of the Steamboat Historical
Society of America)
*Workboat Magazine*. Portland, Maine:
Diversified Business Communications
(monthly)

## Books

Johnson, B. *Foss Maritime—A Living
Legend*. Seattle, Portland, San Francisco,
Long Beach, San Diego: Foss Maritime,
1999.

Laing, Alexander. *The American Heritage of
Seafaring America*. New York: American
Heritage Publishing Co., 1974.

Lang, Steve, and Peter H. Spectre. *On the
Hawser*. Camden, Maine: Down East
Books, 1980.

Newell, Gordon, and Joe Williamson. *Pacific
Tugboats: Parade of Tugs, Ships, and Men*.
Bonanza Books, 1958.

Turner, Robert D. *Sternwheelers & Steam
Tugs: An Illustrated History of the
Canadian Pacific Railway's Columbia
Lake & River Service*. Victoria, British
Columbia: Sono Nis Press, 1998.

# INDEX